Beyond the Veil

A Journey Through Life After Death

PART TWO

What lies beyond is not the end, but a profound continuation.

SHREE SHAMBAV

Beyond the Veil

A Journey Through Life After Death

Shree Shambav

Published by Shree Shambav, Tamil Nadu, India
Shree Shambav Ink & Imagination "Where Words
Breathe and Imagination Soars"
All Rights Reserved
First Edition, 2025

Copyright © 2025, Muniswamy Rajakumar

All rights reserved. No part of this publication may be reproduced, distributed, or transmitted in any form or by any means, including photocopying, recording, or other electronic or mechanical methods, without the author's prior written permission. It is illegal to copy this book, post it to a website, or distribute it by any other means without permission.

The request for permission should be addressed to the author.

ISBN: 978-93-342-5656-7

Email:shreeshambav@gmail.com

Web:www.shambav.org

DEDICATION

"Isavasyam idam sarvam yat kim ca jagatyam jagat, tena tyaktena bhunjitha, ma gridhah kasyasvid dhanam"

To the Almighty,

the Divine Masters,

the family who listens,

and my parents who see –

your presence shapes the pages of my life's journey.

"Isavasyam idam sarvam yat kim ca jagatyam jagat"

Meaning: "God encompasses everything you perceive, see, or touch with your sense organs."

DISCLAIMER

Beyond the Veil: A Journey Through Life After Death explores humanity's timeless curiosity about what happens after death through philosophical, spiritual, and scientific perspectives. This book invites readers to delve into the profound nature of consciousness and its transformative potential. While the journey may evoke moments of deep insight and reflection, it may also challenge deeply held beliefs or stir strong emotional responses. These reactions are part of the natural process of self-discovery and growth.

If you experience emotional distress, confusion, or discomfort while engaging with the material, we encourage you to seek guidance from a licensed therapist, counsellor, or other qualified professional. Prioritising your emotional well-being is essential as you navigate this exploration.

The practices and exercises included in this book are suggestions to enhance spiritual and personal development. As every individual's experiences and needs are unique, readers are encouraged to adapt these practices to suit their personal journeys, proceeding at a pace that feels comfortable. Personal growth is a deeply individual process, and outcomes will vary based on your engagement, readiness, and circumstances.

The author and publisher disclaim any liability for direct or indirect outcomes resulting from the application of the concepts, practices, or insights shared in this book. By engaging with this material, you acknowledge and accept personal responsibility for your own transformation, mindfulness, and discernment.

This book does not promise specific results but serves as an invitation to explore the infinite potential within yourself. Take what resonates with your journey, leave what does not, and trust your innate capacity for healing, growth, and wisdom.

We are honoured to accompany you on this journey of awakening to the infinite. May the insights offered here inspire you to live with greater clarity, purpose, and connection. May this book act as a catalyst for profound transformation and a deeper understanding of yourself, your soul, and the mysteries of existence.

Note - If any part of the book, in any sequence, hurts the reader's sentiments, it would be just out of a sheer accident, not intentional

EPIGRAM

Beyond the Veil

"Death is not an end, nor a silence—it is the gentle turning of a page, the breath of a soul unburdened by its earthly name. Beyond the veil, where time melts into eternity, and form fades into memory, consciousness awakens to its infinite essence. In that boundless expanse, the soul remembers—it was never lost, never alone, and never truly gone."

– Shree Shambav

Beyond the Veil

A Journey Through Life After Death

Shree Shambav

Shree Shambav is a 26x best-selling author renowned for his transformative works in personal development and spiritual growth.

Dear Cherished Readers

Dear Cherished Readers,

As I embark on this new literary voyage, my heart swells with profound gratitude and an overwhelming sense of connection. With deep emotion, I extend my heartfelt appreciation to each of you who has joined me on this journey.

With sincere warmth, I invite you to revisit the steps we have taken together through the pages of my earlier works. Our odyssey began with "Journey of Soul - Karma," a book that marked my first foray into the world of words and a testament to the raw passion that ignited my writing adventure.

The subsequent chapters of our shared narrative unfolded through the enchanting tapestry of the "Twenty + One" series, both Series I and Series II. Each page turned was a brushstroke on the canvas of our imaginations, painting vivid stories that I hoped would resonate deeply within your hearts.

And how can I forget the transformative journey we embarked on with the "Life Changing Journey— Inspirational Quotes Series?" Day by day, quote by quote, we delved into reflections that uplifted and inspired us and sought to bring a glimpse of light to our souls.

The release of "Death - Light of Life and the Shadow of Death" promises to shed new light on the timeless mystery of death. Similarly, "Unleashing the Incredible Potential of Programming with Python - Optimum - PYTHON: Ultimate Guide for Beginners Series I" is poised to empower readers with newfound knowledge.

In addition, my technical book, OPTIMUM Python Series II - Exploring Data Structures and Algorithms, delves into advanced concepts in Python programming, offering a comprehensive guide for those seeking to deepen their understanding.

Shree Shambav expands his artistic repertoire with "*Whispers of Eternity: 150 Plus - A Symphony of Soulful Verses*," a heartfelt exploration of the human experience. Alongside this, his "*Whispers of the Soul: A Journey Through Haiku*" distils profound insights into poignant verses. Together, these works showcase his versatility and mastery of soulful expression, inviting readers on a journey of self-discovery. Through his poetry, he weaves a rich tapestry of emotion that resonates deeply with the heart.

Shree Shambav's latest works—*Learn to Love Yourself: A Journey of Discovering Inner Beauty and Strength Through*

10 Transformative Rules, The Power of Letting Go: Embrace Freedom and Happiness, A Journey of Lasting Peace—are true treasures of self-discovery, The Entitlement Trap: Get Over It, Get On, Whispers of a Dying Soul: Unspoken Regrets and Unlived Dreams, Whispers of Silence - Unlocking Inner Power through Stillness, The Power of Words: Transforming Speech, Transforming Lives, and Awakening the Infinite: The Power of Consciousness in Transforming Life. Each book offers profound insights into personal growth and well-being, guiding readers on a transformative journey toward inner peace and fulfilment.

In addition to these works, Shree Shambav has recently ventured into astrology with the release of Astrology Unveiled – Foundations of Ancient Wisdom Series I to VI, expanding into the realm of metaphysics. These books explore the foundational principles of Vedic astrology, offering readers a rich and practical understanding of this ancient wisdom.

Your unwavering support, enthusiasm to immerse yourself in my writings, and readiness to embark on these journeys with me have been my greatest sources of inspiration. Your input has been a beacon guiding me through the creation process, moulding these stories into containers of passion, emotion, knowledge, and resonance.

As I unveil this new narrative before you, know that your presence, insights, and shared moments have been my companions. The path we have walked together is etched in the annals of my creative evolution, and it's an honour beyond words to have you by my side once more.

Here's to the readers who have illuminated my path with their presence, who have embraced my stories with open hearts, and who have woven themselves into the very fabric of my literary world. Our journey has been a symbiotic dance of writer and reader, a harmony of souls brought together by the magic of storytelling.

With a heart brimming with appreciation and eyes glistening with anticipation, I extend my deepest gratitude for your unwavering support. Thank you for the memories, the shared emotions, and the countless hours spent in the worlds we've crafted together. As we step into this new adventure, let's continue to explore, feel, and discover the boundless horizons that words can unveil.

Warmly,

Shree Shambav

BEYOND THE VEIL

Suggested Reads

FROM BEST-SELLING AUTHOR

Endorsements

"Beyond the Veil is a masterful and thought-provoking exploration of life's greatest mystery—what happens after we die? With a rare blend of spiritual insight, scientific inquiry, and philosophical depth, this book invites readers to journey beyond the limits of the physical world and into the vast possibilities of consciousness. Rich with wisdom, compelling accounts, and profound reflections, it offers solace, inspiration, and a deeper understanding of the eternal nature of existence. A must-read for anyone seeking clarity, comfort, or a new perspective on the afterlife."

— Mrs Nandini, Educationist

About the Author

Shree Shambav is a visionary luminary—an internationally acclaimed best-selling author, inspirational speaker, artist, philanthropist, life coach, and entrepreneur. A world record holder, his deep passion for music led him to create soul-stirring albums, drawing inspiration from his celebrated poetry collection, Whispers of Eternity. With wisdom and grace, he has transformed countless lives through his counseling, teachings, and writings, guiding individuals toward profound personal growth and self-discovery.

A 26-time best-selling author, Shree Shambav is renowned for his insightful contributions to personal development and spiritual awakening. His work continues to uplift and inspire, offering timeless wisdom that empowers individuals to embrace their true potential.

Shree Shambav's literary journey took flight with the celebrated Journey of Soul - Karma, where he delved into the depths of human experience to unveil profound insights. Garnering recognition through multiple literature awards, his repertoire includes esteemed works, such as the Twenty + One Series and the enlightening Life Changing Journey – Inspirational Quotes series.

As a distinguished alumnus of the Indian Institute of Management and the National Institute of Technology, Shree Shambav brings a wealth of corporate acumen from his tenure in multinational corporations. His most recent publications, including Unveiling the Enigma, Death - Light of Life and the Shadow of Death and Optimum - Python Series I and Series II, demonstrate his mastery of both the literary and technical spheres.

Shree Shambav expands his artistic repertoire with "*Whispers of Eternity: 150 Plus - A Symphony of Soulful Verses*," a heartfelt exploration of the human experience. Alongside this, his "*Whispers of the Soul: A Journey Through Haiku*" distils profound insights into poignant verses. Together, these works showcase his versatility and mastery of soulful expression, inviting readers on a journey of self-discovery. Through his poetry, he weaves a rich tapestry of emotion that resonates deeply with the heart.

Shree Shambav's latest works—*Learn to Love Yourself: A Journey of Discovering Inner Beauty and Strength Through 10 Transformative Rules, The Power of Letting Go: Embrace Freedom and Happiness, A Journey of Lasting Peace*—are true treasures of self-discovery, *The Entitlement Trap: Get Over It, Get On, Whispers of a Dying Soul: Unspoken Regrets and Unlived Dreams, Whispers of Silence - Unlocking Inner Power through Stillness* and *The Power of Words: Transforming Speech, Transforming Lives.* Each book offers profound insights into personal growth and well-being, guiding readers on a transformative journey toward inner peace and fulfilment.

In addition to these works, Shree Shambav has recently ventured into astrology with the release of Astrology Unveiled – Foundations of Ancient Wisdom Series I to VI, expanding into the realm of metaphysics. These books explore the foundational principles of Vedic astrology, offering readers a rich and practical understanding of this ancient wisdom.

Shree Shambav established the Ayur Rakshita Foundation, which is dedicated to promoting boundless growth, universal fraternity, and environmental protection. The charity helps diverse communities while working for societal progress.

To learn more about Shree Shambav and his works, visit his website at www.shambav.org. For information about the Ayur Rakshita Foundation and its initiatives, visit www.shambav-ayurrakshita.org.

Let's Follow him on Social Media: **@shreeshambav**

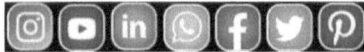

PREFACE

From the moment we are born, we begin an inevitable journey toward the unknown. The question of what lies beyond the threshold of death has lingered in the human heart for as long as we have existed. It is a question whispered in moments of silence, pondered in the solitude of night, and shared across cultures, faiths, and generations. Death is our one certainty, yet it remains cloaked in mystery. What happens when we die? Is it the end or merely the beginning of something greater?

This book, *Beyond the Veil: A Journey Through Life After Death,* invites you to join an exploration of one of humanity's most profound questions. It is not a journey of conclusions but of inquiry—an effort to bridge the seen and unseen, the material and the spiritual, the scientific and the mystical. Together, we will delve into perspectives that span centuries and civilisations, seeking not definitive answers, but a richer understanding of what it means to live, to die, and to exist beyond.

Death is often approached with fear, but within its mystery lies profound wisdom. It is a teacher, reminding us of life's impermanence and urging us to live with greater purpose and authenticity. Through its lens, we begin to see what truly matters—love, connection, growth, and the evolution of the soul. To reflect on death is not to dwell in despair, but to awaken to the beauty and fragility of the present moment.

This book is structured into two parts, encompassing six sections, each offering a profound exploration of life, death, and the mysteries beyond. Due to its depth and scope, Part One covers the first three sections, while Part Two delves into the remaining three.

The journey begins with an exploration of death and consciousness. What is death, truly? Is it an end or a transition? How have different cultures and spiritual traditions understood it across time? We will question whether consciousness is bound to the body or if it transcends the physical realm, leading us into scientific investigations of near-death experiences, reincarnation, and the soul's journey beyond earthly existence.

The middle sections serve as a bridge between science and spirituality, unravelling the intricate connections between karma, consciousness, and the afterlife. Through personal accounts, ancient wisdom, and modern research, we will explore what may unfold immediately after death—the realms of the interlife and the soul's continuing evolution.

In the final sections, the focus shifts inward, inviting deep reflection on how an awareness of mortality can transform the way we live. How does embracing impermanence influence our choices, relationships, and spiritual growth? What practices can help us prepare for a peaceful transition when the time comes? And how can the mysteries that remain beyond our grasp inspire a life filled with faith, wonder, and gratitude?

Beyond being an inquiry into what happens after we die, this book is a guide to living with deeper meaning, purpose, and a greater connection to the eternal.

This book is not a doctrine, nor is it a promise of what lies beyond. Instead, it is a collection of insights, reflections, and questions meant to inspire your own exploration. It invites you to step into the unknown with curiosity and courage, to embrace the mystery of existence, and to find meaning in the eternal dance of life and death.

As you turn these pages, you may find ideas that challenge your beliefs, affirm your experiences, or awaken something new within you. Allow yourself the grace to sit with these questions, for they are not meant to be solved but lived. The journey through life, death, and the afterlife is deeply personal, and the path you walk is uniquely your own.

May this book serve as a companion and guide, offering clarity where there is doubt, peace where there is fear, and hope where there is uncertainty. Beyond the veil lies a vast and infinite mystery, but within it, we may find the essence of who we are.

Welcome to the exploration. May it deepen your connection to yourself, to others, and to the eternal thread that binds us all.

With gratitude and encouragement,

Shree Shambav

INTRODUCTION

The Eternal Question

Since the dawn of humanity, we have looked to the heavens, the earth, and one another in search of answers to the question that shadows every human life: *What happens after death?*

This question is neither new nor obscure. It is perhaps the most universal and timeless of all inquiries—one that has shaped civilisations, inspired spiritual traditions, and stirred the hearts of seekers across generations. It is a question that lingers in quiet moments, that whispers through grief and loss, and that ultimately leads us to the very edge of what we can comprehend. Death is the great equaliser, the inevitable passage that unites all beings, yet its true nature remains shrouded in mystery.

Is death an end or a transformation? A threshold to another existence or a return to the infinite? Are we merely biological beings, or is there something eternal within us—a consciousness, a soul, a spark that transcends the physical world? The veil that separates the known from the unknown is thin, yet beyond it lies a vast and unfathomable expanse.

In *Beyond the Veil: A Journey Through Life After Death*, we embark on a profound exploration of these mysteries. This is not a journey to provide absolute answers—for the afterlife, by its very nature, defies certainty. Rather, this book is an invitation: to wonder, to question, and to embrace the unknown with open hearts and minds. We will weave together philosophy, spiritual wisdom, scientific inquiry, and personal accounts to illuminate what may lie beyond our final breath.

This journey begins with an exploration of death itself—its biological, philosophical, and spiritual dimensions. Across cultures and traditions, perspectives on death range from the finality of the material body to the immortality of the soul. Science, too, has ventured into this enigmatic realm, studying near-death experiences, consciousness, and the possibility of an existence beyond physicality. Though science and spirituality have often been seen as opposing forces, we will seek to bridge them, revealing the ways in which they converge to offer profound insights into the nature of existence.

As we delve deeper, we will explore the soul's journey as described by ancient traditions, the role of consciousness in shaping reality, and the experiences of those who claim to have glimpsed the other side.

Near-death experiences, deathbed visions, and past-life memories challenge our conventional understanding of mortality, while teachings on karma, reincarnation, and enlightenment invite us to consider the possibility of a soul evolving across lifetimes.

Yet, this journey is not solely about what happens after death. It is, perhaps more importantly, about the lessons that death teaches us about life. When we embrace our impermanence, we begin to understand the urgency of living with authenticity, purpose, and love. Death, rather than being an adversary to be feared, becomes a teacher—one that reminds us to cherish each fleeting moment, to nurture meaningful connections, and to align our lives with what truly matters.

As you turn these pages, you may find yourself challenged, comforted, or inspired. You may encounter ideas that resonate deeply or others that provoke new questions. This is the nature of exploring the unknown—it is a deeply personal and transformative process. The goal of this journey is not to impose certainty but to expand awareness, to ignite curiosity, and to deepen our connection to the infinite.

Perhaps, in the end, it is not the answer to the eternal question that matters most. Perhaps, instead, it is the courage to ask, the willingness to seek, and the openness to embrace the great mystery itself.

Let us begin.

With warmth and sincerity,

Shree Shambav

PROLOGUE

There is a moment in every life—a fleeting whisper of awareness—when the certainty of mortality becomes undeniable. Perhaps it comes in the stillness of the night, as shadows stretch long against the wall. Or perhaps it emerges in the depths of grief, as we bid farewell to a loved one and realise that they have ventured into a realm we cannot yet follow. In these moments, we are confronted with the ultimate unknown: death.

What lies beyond this life we hold so dear? Is death a final curtain call, an ending etched in stone? Or is it a gateway, a transition into something vast, luminous, and eternal? For as long as humanity has existed, we have sought to peer beyond the veil, yearning for answers to questions that are both profoundly personal and universally shared.

The stories of those who claim to have glimpsed the other side—through near-death experiences, past-life memories, or mystical visions—offer tantalising hints of continuity. Ancient spiritual traditions have passed down teachings of rebirth, heavenly realms, and ultimate liberation. At the same time, science has begun its own exploration of consciousness and the mysteries of the mind, daring to ask whether death is truly the end or merely a transformation.

This prologue is a bridge between two worlds: the tangible and the transcendent. It is an invitation to journey with open minds and open hearts, knowing that the path ahead will be one of exploration, not certainty; of wonder, not answers.

Death is not a subject we easily embrace. It stirs fear, discomfort, and resistance, even as it beckons us with the promise of understanding. Yet it is in facing death that we begin to truly grasp the beauty and fragility of life. Every culture, every belief system, and every individual has approached this enigma with their own lens, weaving together a tapestry of perspectives that is as diverse as humanity itself.

In Parts One and Two of this book series, we embark on a profound exploration of death—not as an end, but as a gateway to deeper understanding. We will delve into the biological realities of dying, the spiritual traditions that illuminate the soul's journey, and the scientific inquiries that challenge the very limits of human knowledge. Along the way, we will listen to the voices of those who have ventured to the threshold of life and returned with stories that defy explanation—accounts that blur the line between the physical and the transcendent.

This journey is not about seeking simple answers but about embracing the vastness of the unknown. We will ask questions that have no definitive resolution and sit within the mystery, allowing its paradoxes and profundities to unfold. Through this, we may come to see death not as a final curtain but as a transformation—one that calls us to live with greater awareness, meaning, and reverence for the unseen threads that weave through existence.

But this journey is not merely an academic or philosophical pursuit. It is deeply personal. To understand death is to understand life—to see its preciousness, its impermanence, and its interconnectedness with the infinite. To explore what lies beyond is to reflect on our own purpose, our relationships, and the legacy we leave behind.

The veil that separates life from death is thin, yet it is often impenetrable. In its presence, we are reminded of our limitations but also of our boundless capacity for wonder. What lies beyond may remain a mystery, but the act of seeking it enriches our lives in ways that are both profound and transformative.

As you embark on this journey *Beyond the Veil*, I invite you to bring your curiosity, your doubts, and your hopes. Together, let us walk the path toward understanding—not to find definitive answers but to deepen our connection to the eternal questions that unite us all.

Let us dare to look beyond, for in doing so, we may discover not only what lies after death but what it truly means to live.

Welcome to the Beyond the Veil: A Journey Through Life After Death.

CONTENTS

DEDICATION iii

DISCLAIMER v

EPIGRAM vii

Dear Cherished Readers xi

Suggested Reads xv

Endorsements xvii

About the Author xix

PREFACE xxiii

INTRODUCTION xxvii

PROLOGUE xxxi

At Kanchipuram 1

  A Journey Beyond Fear 1

  The Silence That Speaks 7

    Whispers Beyond the Veil 13

  SECTION ONE 41

    Evidence and Experiences 41

  CHAPTER 1 43

    Communicating with the Departed 43

  CHAPTER II 71

    Is Reincarnation Real? Evidence and Insights ... 71

  CHAPTER III 109

- The Soul's Ultimate Destination 109
- **SECTION TWO** 137
  - Embracing Death as a Teacher 137
- **CHAPTER IV** 139
  - Life Lessons from Death 139
- **CHAPTER V** 161
  - Preparing for the Journey Beyond 161
- **CHAPTER VI** 197
  - Unanswered Questions and the Mystery of the Infinite 197
- **SECTION THREE** 231
  - A Reflection 231
- **CHAPTER VII** 233
  - Embracing the Eternal 233
- **WRAP UP** 273
  - A Journey Through Life After Death 273
- **Life Coach and Philanthropist** 281
- **TESTIMONIALS** 285
- **ACKNOWLEDGEMENTS** 293
- **BOOKS BY - AUTHOR** 295

BEYOND THE VEIL

At Kanchipuram
A Journey Beyond Fear

"The soul does not fear the unknown; it longs for it, for beyond the veil lies not an end, but the great unfolding of all that was, is, and will be."

- *Shree Shambav*

The dawn embraced the ashram with quiet majesty, and the sky cloaked in twilight hues as the cool morning breeze caressed the earth. Leaves danced to a rhythm only nature could compose, their soft rustle blending seamlessly with the silence that reigned. Beneath the sprawling canopy of an ancient banyan tree, Akshaya, Vasudeva, and Vidyarthi sat in profound meditation, their forms as still as statues, their breaths merging with the pulse of the universe.

Elsewhere in the ashram, figures moved like whispers in the pre-dawn light. Some journeyed toward the Zen Meditation Centre, their footsteps purposeful yet serene. Others were already lost in the flow of yoga, their bodies bending and stretching in perfect harmony with the awakening earth.

Nita, Lalitha, and Rohith emerged from the meditation hall, their souls still wrapped in the lingering stillness of deep contemplation. As they moved through the ashram grounds, they met Sujitha and Espen, who greeted them with quiet smiles, as if words would disturb the sanctity of the moment. Together, they walked along the stone pathways, winding past the flowering gardens, the scent of jasmine and incense mingling in the cool morning air.

A deep resonance soon stirred the silence—the chanting of "OM" filled the air, reverberating like a heartbeat through the ashram walls. The sacred syllable spread across the landscape, merging with the soft echoes of nature's own song. Soon, the melodic hum of bhajans intertwined with the rhythm, accompanied by the rich timbre of tabla, dholak, cymbals, harmonium, mridangam, and other sacred instruments. The atmosphere transformed, alive with devotion and energy, as if the divine itself had descended to join in the symphony.

After their morning meditation, Akshaya and the others rose slowly, their movements mindful and deliberate. Together, they walked toward the Shambav Bhajan Hall, where the voices of Apeksha and Akshatha soared, deeply immersed in their morning devotion. Passing through the garden paths, they saw Roopa, Abhilasha, Abhirami, Alice, and Sofia gracefully flowing through their yoga postures, their focus unbroken even as the music filled the air. Nita and the others joined them, moving fluidly into asanas that aligned their breath with the universe itself.

As the sun ascended higher, painting the sky in strokes of orange and gold, the group gathered beneath another sacred tree in the heart of Brindavan Garden. The tree stood like a sentinel, its branches spreading wide, offering shade and shelter as if blessing the assembly. Astyn, Kieron, Sam, and Bhavya joined them, settling onto the soft earth. The fog lingered gently, shrouding the surroundings in a mystical veil, while the trees seemed to sway in rhythm with the dholak's beat, their leaves vibrating as though attuned to the divine energy permeating the space. Devotees passed by, their voices harmonising in songs of devotion, their spirits soaring with every chant.

Kieron stretched his legs and exhaled deeply, glancing at the sky. "Finally, we are here, waiting for Guruji's session."

Nita clasped her hands together, her eyes brimming with quiet joy. "Yes… I was just waiting for this day."

The rest nodded in silent agreement, anticipation thick in the air.

Then, Akshaya spoke, his voice carrying the weight of remembrance. "I still remember my last retreat here," he said softly, his gaze distant as if looking into another lifetime.

The group turned their attention toward him, their curiosity piqued.

"I had come seeking answers," Akshaya continued, his tone laced with quiet reverence. "But what I received was far beyond anything I had expected. I remember sitting right here, beneath this very tree, watching the way the morning mist clung to the earth, how the sun's first light turned everything to gold. I remember how, at first, I carried so many questions—about life, about death, about what lies beyond. And then, Guruji arrived."

His voice softened as if speaking of something sacred. "He walked in silence, yet his presence was thunderous. He sat before us, his gaze sweeping over each of us as if he could see straight into our souls. He didn't speak for a long time. We simply sat in the quiet, listening to the birds, the wind, and the rustling of the leaves. And then, finally, he asked us: What is it that truly dies?"

Akshaya paused, letting the question settle over the group.

"At that moment, I realised how little I truly understood. We speak of death as if it were the end, yet Guruji's words made me question everything. What is it that dies? The body? The name? The stories we tell ourselves? But what of consciousness? What of that presence within us that feels, that witnesses, that exists beyond time? I remember sitting there, my heart pounding, as Guruji spoke about how we live our lives clinging to identities that are as fleeting as shadows. How we mourn endings without recognising that within every ending is the seed of something eternal."

A hush had fallen over the group, the weight of Akshaya's words sinking deep into their hearts.

"That day," Akshaya continued, "I learned that death is not darkness. It is a doorway. Not an end, but a transition. And in that realisation, I felt something within me shift—like a veil lifting. Fear dissolved. Not entirely, not yet, but enough for me to see that life, in all its fleeting beauty, is a gift. That the fear of death is, in truth, the fear of an unlived life."

Silence followed his words, profound and full. The wind whispered through the leaves as if carrying his message through the ashram.

Finally, Kiran gently interrupted the moment. "Let's prepare for breakfast. The day ahead is full, and Guruji's session awaits."

Akshaya and the others smiled and nodded, leading the group toward the Annapoorneswari facility, where the aroma of freshly prepared food filled the air. The hall was abuzz with quiet joy as devotees gathered, their faces glowing with gratitude.

Astyn inhaled deeply, her eyes alight with pleasure. "The aroma is heavenly."

"Come, let's eat," Akshaya suggested warmly.

The group settled down to share their meal, a sense of peace and purpose enveloping them. Every bite seemed infused with gratitude; every word spoken was laced with joy. They were not merely individuals gathered at an ashram—they were seekers on a shared journey, each step bringing them closer to the eternal truths they yearned to uncover.

The Silence That Speaks

"The journey is not about reaching a destination, but about dissolving the illusion of separation—awakening to the eternal oneness that has always been." – Shree Shambav.

The soft rustling of robes and the faint echo of footsteps marked Guruji's arrival into the serene embrace of the Buddha Hall. The air itself seemed to shift as if recognising the presence of a soul, and a gentle hush settled over the gathering. The golden morning light streamed through the stained-glass windows, casting ethereal patterns upon the polished floor, illuminating dust motes that danced like celestial beings in the stillness. It was as though time had momentarily bowed in reverence, pausing to honour the sacred unfolding of this moment.

Each devotee instinctively lowered their gaze, hands folded in Atma Namaste, their hearts swelling with devotion, reverence, and quiet anticipation. Some closed their eyes, drinking in the sanctity of the moment, while others simply surrendered to the serenity that Guruji's presence exuded. His aura was both weightless and immense—a paradox of grace and power, as if the wisdom of ages had distilled itself into the gentle curve of his smile, the measured cadence of his breath.

Moving with effortless stillness, Guruji approached the centre of the hall and took his asana, his posture a seamless blend of ease and purpose. There was something about his presence that was beyond physicality—it was as if he was not merely sitting but becoming one with the space itself. The room, the moment, the seekers—all seemed to dissolve into the quiet vastness that surrounded him.

He closed his eyes, and in that instant, the silence deepened. It was not an empty silence but one pregnant with meaning, like the pause between musical notes that gives melody its depth. He sat there, utterly still, as if listening to the whisper of the cosmos, attuning himself to the eternal rhythm that underlies all existence. In that sacred stillness, the devotees felt something shift within themselves—a subtle stirring, a beckoning toward something greater, something unseen yet profoundly felt.

Minutes passed, though time itself felt irrelevant in the sanctity of that space. When Guruji finally opened his eyes, they were luminous, carrying the weight of countless journeys and the tenderness of a thousand suns. His gaze, soft yet penetrating, swept across the hall, meeting each soul with an unspoken knowing, a quiet recognition of the eternal within them. It was not just a look; it was an embrace, a reminder, a homecoming.

At that moment, the question of seeking dissolved. There were no barriers, no separations—just the simple, undeniable truth that something sacred, something infinite, had always been there, waiting to be remembered.

With an enigmatic smile, Guruji turned to Vasudeva. "Did Gandhari ever see her sons during her lifetime?"

Vasudeva hesitated, his mind searching for an answer in the depths of memory but finding none. The uncertainty flickered in his eyes.

Guruji's gaze held the patience of centuries. "Once," he said softly, "just once, after the great war had ended, Gandhari saw her sons—years after they had perished on the battlefield. It was not in the world of the living, nor in the realm of dreams, but in a space between, where time bends, and the soul speaks its truest language."

The mention of Mahabharata Anushasana Parva (Book of Instructions) stirred something profound within the listeners. Guruji's voice deepened, carrying them across the river of time to the banks of the sacred Bhagirathi, where the great sage Vedavyasa stood, his divine presence illuminating the night.

Fifteen years had passed since the Kurukshetra war, yet the wounds it left behind still festered in the hearts of those who had lost everything. The once-mighty king Dhritarashtra, now blind and frail, walked with the weight of a hundred lives lost—the lives of his sons fell in battle. Beside him stood Gandhari, the mother who had bound her own eyes in sacrifice yet had seen more suffering than any mother ever should.

On that night, the waters of Bhagirathi shimmered with an otherworldly glow. With the power of his penance, Vedavyasa summoned forth the spirits of the warriors lost to war. One by one, they emerged—Karna, his armour no longer shielding him from the embrace of those who had once shunned him. Duryodhana, standing with the pride of a prince but without the fire of enmity. Dushasana, whose hands no longer dripped with Draupadi's dishonour but instead glowed with the light of a soul freed from its burdens.

And there they were—the hundred Kauravas, their once-mortal forms now clad in celestial garments, their brows no longer creased with ambition or rivalry. They stood in a luminous assembly, no longer warriors, no longer bound by the sins and virtues of their past lives. Their weapons were gone, and their chariots turned to mist. What remained was pure essence—souls stripped of anger, of vengeance, of grief.

For the first time in her life, Gandhari saw her sons—not as fallen warriors, not as the architects of destruction, but as they truly were: radiant, free, and unburdened. In that sacred moment, there was no war, no loss—only reunion. She and Dhritarashtra spent the night speaking with them, their words no longer carrying sorrow but the tenderness of a mother's love, of a father's longing.

Guruji's voice softened, carrying the weight of a thousand meanings. "Do you see, Vasudeva? Life and death are not divided by an impenetrable wall. They are but two shores of the same river. And sometimes, if the current is still if the heart is open, the veil's part, and we glimpse the truth—that love, that longing, that connection… it never truly dies."

The listeners sat motionless, their breaths stolen by the sheer depth of the story. In that moment, the ashram itself felt like a sacred river, flowing with time, memory, and a truth too profound to be spoken outright.

Vasudeva finally exhaled, his eyes glistening with the weight of understanding. "So, even in death, there is a reunion," he murmured.

Guruji smiled, the wisdom of the ages twinkling in his eyes. "Not just reunion, Vasudeva… realisation. The realisation that all separation is an illusion. That love transcends lifetimes. That the ones we grieve are never truly lost."

Whispers Beyond the Veil

"True wisdom is not found in the noise of knowledge, but in the silence of understanding—where the soul listens, and the universe speaks."

– Shree Shambav

The Art of Communicating with the Departed

The hall was wrapped in stillness, the air thick with contemplation. Guruji's words hung in the space between thought and inquiry, his presence anchoring the seekers who had gathered. He had just posed the question—a question that had whispered through the corridors of time, a question that had unsettled sceptics and comforted the bereaved: *Can the living truly communicate with the departed?*

Apeksha, who had always been drawn to the mystical, straightened slightly. She had read accounts of near-death experiences, of ethereal visions, of people who claimed to have touched the unseen. And now, Guruji's voice was like a river, flowing through the landscape of history, washing over doubt, carrying the weight of ancient wisdom.

The Shadows on the Cave Wall – A Platonic Reflection

Guruji closed his eyes for a moment, as if drawing from a deeper well of knowledge. "The way we perceive the spiritual world," he began, "is much like Plato's allegory of the cave. Most people live their lives seeing only shadows on the wall, mistaking them for reality. But what if, beyond those shadows, a greater truth awaited? What if the souls of the departed were not gone but merely existed in a reality that our limited senses could not easily grasp?"

The seekers listened intently as Guruji continued, weaving insights from different spiritual traditions.

The Veil Between the Living and the Departed: A Christian Perspective

Guruji's voice carried a quiet reverence as he spoke of the Christian understanding of the departed. Apeksha leaned forward, drawn into the depth of his words, her mind wandering to the countless stories she had encountered—stories of visions, apparitions, and divine encounters that defied logical explanation.

"In Christianity," Guruji continued, "death is not viewed as an end but as a transition into eternal life. The Bible does not speak of the dead as lost, but rather as alive in Christ, part of what is known as 'the communion of saints.'" He paused, allowing the gravity of the words to settle. "The Book of Hebrews 12:1 describes this vividly:

'Therefore, since we are surrounded by such a great cloud of witnesses, let us throw off everything that hinders and the sin that so easily entangles, and let us run with perseverance the race marked out for us.'

"This 'cloud of witnesses' refers to the saints, prophets, and faithful who have departed yet remain spiritually present, offering guidance, interceding for the living, and acting as unseen companions on the journey of faith."

Apeksha felt a shiver run through her as she considered the idea—not just as a poetic metaphor but as a lived reality for many believers.

Apparitions and Visitations: Divine Messages from Beyond

The history of Christianity is rich with accounts of the departed manifesting to the living. Guruji's voice softened as he spoke of these sacred encounters.

"There are those who, in moments of suffering or prayer, have seen their loved ones appear to them—not as mere memories, but as radiant beings of light. There are mystics and saints who have testified to the presence of those beyond the veil, delivering messages of hope, warning, or divine revelation."

Apeksha immediately thought of the many recorded Marian apparitions—manifestations of the Virgin Mary to the faithful. The most famous among them stood as undeniable pillars of Christian mysticism:

Our Lady of Guadalupe (1531) – In Mexico, the Virgin Mary is said to have appeared to a humble indigenous man, Juan Diego, leaving behind an image on his cloak that science has struggled to explain.

Our Lady of Lourdes (1858) – A young girl, Bernadette Soubirous, witnessed the Virgin Mary in a grotto in France, where healing waters began to flow. To this day, Lourdes remains a sacred pilgrimage site.

Our Lady of Fatima (1917) – Three shepherd children in Portugal received visions of Mary, along with prophetic messages and a celestial phenomenon witnessed by thousands.

"These are not merely legends," Guruji explained, his voice carrying the weight of centuries of belief. "The Catholic Church investigates such events with great scrutiny, requiring extensive evidence before declaring an apparition as authentic."

The Saints and the Living: Intercessors Beyond Time

Guruji turned his gaze to the seekers before him. "In Catholic and Orthodox Christianity, the saints are not viewed as distant figures of history but as living souls who continue their divine mission beyond death. They are believed to intercede on behalf of those who pray to them, much like a friend or a mentor guiding you from afar."

Apeksha thought of the thousands of stories she had read—testimonies of people who had prayed to St. Anthony and miraculously found lost items or those who sought St. Padre Pio's intercession and experienced healing beyond medical explanation.

Guruji continued, "The Bible provides glimpses of this spiritual connection. In the Gospel of Matthew 17:1-3, Jesus is seen speaking with Moses and Elijah during the Transfiguration—two prophets who had long departed the earthly realm yet were fully present in the moment."

The realisation struck Apeksha with force. If even Christ spoke with those who had passed, was it not possible that the departed could still reach out to the living?

Dreams, Visions, and Mystical Encounters

"Many believers," Guruji said, "have shared that their departed loved ones visit them in dreams, not as fleeting memories but as conscious presences delivering messages of comfort or unfinished business. These experiences are often transformative, leaving the dreamer with an undeniable sense of peace."

He referenced the story of **St. Monica**, the mother of St. Augustine, who prayed tirelessly for her wayward son. In her sorrow, she had a vision where a divine messenger assured her that her son would return to faith. Years later, Augustine became one of Christianity's greatest theologians, a testament to the power of spiritual connection beyond life and death.

Even in more modern accounts, people report receiving warnings, reassurances, or even a sense of protection from loved ones who have passed. Was this simply the subconscious mind offering solace? Or did the soul indeed reach across the veil?

Skepticism and Faith: The Eternal Debate

"Of course," Guruji acknowledged, "not all accept these encounters as truth. Sceptics argue that such experiences are psychological, mere echoes of grief. Science seeks tangible proof, yet the nature of the soul remains beyond its grasp."

He smiled gently. "But does absence of proof mean absence of existence? Love, after all, is unseen—yet we do not question its reality. Why, then, should the presence of the departed be dismissed so easily?"

The Bridge Between Realms

Apeksha's heart was restless. The idea that the dead could remain connected to the living was not just a comforting thought—it was a bridge between worlds. A whisper in the silence. A presence felt but unseen.

Guruji said, "Perhaps the departed never truly leave us. Perhaps they exist in a space just beyond our perception, guiding, watching, waiting—until the day when we, too, step beyond the veil."

Buddhism and Zen: The Impermanence of Boundaries

Guruji's gaze was steady as he spoke. The seekers before him sat motionless, their hearts and minds absorbing the depth of his words. "Buddhism teaches that the boundary between life and death is an illusion," he said, his voice calm as a still pond. "We see them as opposites, yet are they truly separate? Zen masters often ask—when a wave rises from the ocean and then dissolves back into it, has it died? Or has it merely returned to its source?"

If the soul was like a wave, then perhaps death was not an end but merely a return. A return to something vast, something infinite—beyond human comprehension.

The River and the Ocean:

Guruji's voice softened, and he leaned forward slightly. "Let me tell you a story: There was once a young monk who lived by a great river. He would sit by its edge every morning, watching its endless flow. One day, he turned to his master and asked, 'Master, where does the river go?'

The old master smiled and replied, 'It goes to the ocean.'

'And what happens when it reaches the ocean?' the young monk pressed.

The master dipped his fingers into the water, letting a few drops trickle into the river. 'Tell me, where did those drops go? Are they lost? Or have they become one with the river, just as the river becomes one with the ocean?'

The young monk was silent, contemplating the answer.

Guruji let the story linger, allowing his devotees to immerse themselves in its meaning. "Death," he continued, "is not destruction. It is the river meeting the ocean. What you call 'self' dissolves into the vastness of existence. In Zen, this is called **mu**—emptiness that is full, an ending that is not an end."

Apeksha felt a deep stirring within her. If life and death were mere transitions, then what did that mean for the departed? Were they gone—or had they simply become something greater?

The Bardo: A Realm Between Worlds

Guruji's eyes gleamed as he continued, "The Tibetan Book of the Dead—Bardo Thödol—teaches that consciousness does not immediately vanish at death. Instead, it enters the Bardo, an intermediate state between death and rebirth."

A hush settled over the hall as Guruji described the Bardo in vivid detail.

"In this state," he explained, "the soul encounters visions—some beautiful, some terrifying. These are reflections of the mind itself, revealing attachments, fears, and desires. For 49 days, the soul journeys through the Bardo, either moving toward enlightenment or being drawn back into the cycle of rebirth."

He paused, letting the words take root before adding, "Tibetan monks chant sacred prayers during this period—not simply as rituals, but as **guiding lights** for the departed. It is believed that through deep meditation and compassionate intent, the living can aid the dead in their passage. The boundary is not as rigid as we think. Those who have mastered the mind can walk both worlds."

Zen Masters and the Moment of Death

"Zen monks," Guruji continued, "do not fear death. For them, it is but a moment in the great unfolding."

He smiled slightly as if recalling an old friend. "There is a tradition among Zen masters—when they sense their final moment approaching, they compose a death poem—a few final words of insight, a last ripple in the river before it merges with the ocean."

He recited one from the great Zen master Kozan Ichikyo:

"Empty-handed I entered the world,
Barefoot I leave it.
My coming, my going—
Two simple happenings
That got entangled."

Nita's breath caught in her throat. The simplicity. The truth. It was as if the monk had reached through time and whispered directly to her soul.

Guruji, after a pause, said:

No birth, no end, just endless flow,
No gifts to give, no debt to owe.

A silent wave, a fleeting breath—
Farewell, beyond all life and death.

He let the silence linger. There was nothing more to say—because truth does not require explanation.

The Illusion of Separation

Apeksha closed her eyes, her thoughts dissolving like ink in water. She had always feared death—not just her own, but the loss of those she loved. She had clung to memories, to grief, to the idea that the departed were **gone**. But now, a new thought arose.

Had they truly disappeared? Or had they merely returned to something larger?

If a wave dissolves back into the ocean, does it truly vanish? Or does it become the vastness itself?

Her heart trembled with understanding.

Guruji's voice, now gentle as the wind, carried one final truth. "We grieve because we see only the surface. But if we quiet the mind, if we truly **see**, we will understand—there is no farewell. No loss. No separation."

The river and the ocean had always been one.

Sufism: The Language of the Heart

"The Sufis," Guruji began, his eyes reflecting an inner radiance, "believe that the soul does not perish; it simply returns to the Beloved. Death is not an end—it is a homecoming."

He let the words linger, then softly recited:

"Don't grieve.
Anything you lose
Comes round in another form."

The words of Rumi drifted through the air like incense, weaving their way into the hearts of the listeners.

The Eternal Dance of Love

Guruji leaned forward slightly, his voice now carrying the gentle cadence of a lover speaking to the moon. "Sufism is the path of the heart. For the Sufi, love is not just an emotion—it is the very fabric of existence, the divine current that flows through all things. The soul, they say, is a lover, eternally seeking reunion with the Divine. Death, then, is not separation; it is the dissolving of self into the infinite embrace of the Beloved."

Apeksha closed her eyes, absorbing the words. What if death was not a loss but a return? What if it was not darkness but a light too vast for human eyes to behold?

Guruji continued, his voice now rich with emotion. "Many Sufi saints have said that those who live in love do not truly die. Their essence lingers, their presence remains, for love does not obey the laws of time."

Guruji, after a brief pause, said:

Those who love are never gone,
Their light still shines, and their souls live on.
In whispered winds and midnight skies,
Their presence lingers, and love never dies.

No clock can steal, no tide erase,
The touch of love, its soft embrace.
Beyond all time, beyond goodbye,
In love, they live—they do not die.

The Saint Who Spoke Beyond Death

Guruji said, "Let me narrate a story: In a small village in Persia, there lived a Sufi saint named Hazrat Nizam. He was a man of deep devotion, known for his ecstatic poetry and his boundless compassion. His disciples often gathered around him, listening to his words of love and feeling the touch of the Divine in his presence.

But time, as it must, carried him away. He left his body, and his followers were grief-stricken. They could not imagine life without him.

Then, one by one, they began to dream.

One disciple saw him standing beneath the moonlit sky, whispering, *"I have not left you. My love will find you wherever you go."*

Another heard his voice in the wind, calling them by name.

A third, lost in sorrow, felt a gentle hand on their shoulder—though no one was there.

And so, it was. The saint was gone, yet not gone. His presence moved like perfume in the air, unseen yet deeply felt. His love transcended the veil of death."

Guruji's voice softened. "This is what the Sufis mean when they say love is the bridge between worlds. When the heart truly loves, it does not need words, nor does it fear distance. Death does not sever the bond—it only deepens it."

The Whirling Dervish and the Wind

He smiled now as if recalling a vision from another lifetime. "Have you ever seen the Whirling Dervishes?" he asked. "They spin, arms open, lost in the ecstasy of divine love. Do you know why they whirl?"

Sam hesitantly answered, "To connect with God?"

Guruji nodded. "Yes. But also, to disappear."

The hall was silent.

"The dervish spins," Guruji continued, "not to hold on to himself but to dissolve. To become the wind, the sky, the love that moves all things. And in that surrender, there is no birth, no death—only the eternal dance of love."

He paused, his voice turning into a whisper.

"When we mourn the dead, we believe they have left us. But in truth, they have only dissolved into something vaster. If you quiet your heart, if you listen not with your ears but with your soul—you will hear them."

The Presence Beyond Time

Sofia felt her breath catch in her throat. Had she been listening wrong all this time? She had always looked for signs, for words, for proof. But what if the presence of those she had lost was not gone—only beyond the reach of ordinary senses?

What if the language of the departed was not spoken in sound but in love?

Guruji smiled, sensing the shift in the room. "The Sufis say *when a lover truly surrenders, the walls of time and space fall away.* That is why saints appear in dreams, why their presence lingers long after they are gone. Love knows no barriers, no distance. It moves through the unseen, carrying messages across lifetimes."

His gaze swept across the room, holding each seeker in its warmth. "So do not grieve. When love is true, it does not vanish. It only changes form. Listen—not with your mind, but with your heart—and you will hear them."

The seekers sat in stillness, the air thick with something beyond words.

Jainism: The Soul's Journey

Guruji said, "The Jains speak of the soul not as something perishable, but as an eternal traveller," Guruji began, his voice steady, carrying the weight of timeless truth. "Bound by karma, it moves through countless lifetimes, shaping its destiny by thought, word, and deed. Yet, for those who seek the highest truth, there exists a state beyond—one of pure consciousness, where the soul, freed from all bondage, ascends to Siddhashila, never to return to the cycle of birth and death."

The Web of Karma

Guruji continued, "But what of those who remain bound? What of those who pass on, still carrying the weight of unfinished desires, lingering attachments, and unresolved emotions?"

He paused, letting the question settle in the air like a feather drifting to the earth.

"Some souls," he said, "wander between worlds, tethered by longing—seeking closure, seeking release. And it is believed that the living can help them find peace."

The Eternal Devotion of Shravan Kumar

"Let me narrate to you the story of Shravan Kumar," he began, his voice a river flowing through the valley of time. The story had been told countless times, yet each time, it bore new meaning, carrying whispers of devotion, fate, and the unfathomable bonds of love.

Long ago, in a time when dharma was a way of life, there was a young man named Shravan Kumar. Born into humble circumstances, he possessed no riches, no kingdom, no armies to his name. And yet, he was revered far and wide—for his devotion was unparalleled.

His parents, aged and blind, depended on him entirely. But to Shravan, their care was not a burden; it was his sacred duty, the very purpose of his existence. From dawn to dusk, he served them with unwavering love—guiding them with gentle hands, tending to their needs before his own, his heart finding joy in their well-being.

But even the most devoted of sons could not hold back time. His parents longed for one final journey—to visit the holy places, to bathe in the sacred rivers before their souls departed this world.

Shravan, without hesitation, fashioned a kanwar—a balanced yoke with two baskets in which his frail parents could sit. With immense strength, both of body and spirit, he carried them across vast landscapes—through dense forests, across roaring rivers, beneath the scorching sun and the moonlit sky.

Every step was an offering of love.

Every mile, a prayer.

A Tragic Turn of Fate

One day, as they reached the edge of a dense forest, Shravan set his parents down beneath the shade of a great banyan tree. "Rest here, Mother, Father," he said, his voice tender. "I will fetch water for you."

Taking a small vessel, he walked toward the river that flowed nearby, its crystal waters shimmering under the golden light of dusk.

But fate, unseen and unyielding, had already written the next chapter of his story.

Nearby, hidden among the trees, was King Dasharatha, the mighty ruler of Ayodhya. A skilled hunter, he often ventured into the wilderness, his bow ever ready, his senses sharp as an eagle's gaze. That evening, as he waited in silent anticipation, he heard a rustling near the riverbank—a faint gurgling of water, the soft splash of movement.

His instincts took over.

Without hesitation, he drew his bow, the arrow gleaming like lightning, and released it into the unseen darkness.

A single cry shattered the stillness.

Not the roar of a wounded beast.

But the gasp of a man.

Dasharatha rushed forward, his heart pounding. And there, lying by the river's edge, was not a deer, but a young man—his clothes stained crimson, his hands clutching the arrow embedded deep within his chest.

Shravan's breath came in shallow gasps, yet his eyes burned with no anger, no hatred—only sorrow.

"Why... did you do this?" he whispered.

Dasharatha's hands trembled as he knelt beside him. "Forgive me," he pleaded, "I did not see you... I thought—"

Shravan shook his head weakly. "No time... no blame... only one request." His voice was fading, yet the urgency in his eyes remained. "My parents... they wait for me. They are blind... they do not know what has happened. Please... take this water to them. Tell them... their son will not return."

Dasharatha, a mighty king who had never known fear on the battlefield, felt his soul quake at the weight of this moment. He cradled the dying boy in his arms, watching helplessly as Shravan Kumar, the epitome of devotion, took his final breath—not in anger, not in regret, but in a love that transcended even death.

With trembling hands, Dasharatha carried the vessel of water to the old couple.

"Who is there?" the father's frail voice called. "Shravan, my son, is that you?"

Dasharatha's throat tightened. He had faced countless enemies and conquered kingdoms, yet at this moment, he found himself powerless.

He fell to his knees before them and spoke the words that would haunt him for the rest of his days.

"Your son… is no more."

The old couple let out cries of unspeakable grief, their blind eyes filling with tears they could not shed. The weight of their sorrow was unbearable, their pain a wound deeper than any blade could inflict.

With their final breaths, they uttered a curse—a curse that would one day come full circle. "Just as we have lost our son in this cruel manner, you too shall lose yours, and your sorrow will know no end."

And so, the wheel of karma turned.

The Legacy of Shravan Kumar

The story of Shravan Kumar was never forgotten. It became a symbol of **seva**—selfless service, of duty beyond all hardship, of love so profound that even in death, it did not waver.

In every generation, his name was spoken with reverence. In temples, in homes, in the hearts of those who understood that true devotion is not in grand gestures but in the quiet, unwavering sacrifice of one's life for another.

Guruji's voice softened. "Such was the devotion of Shravan Kumar. A soul so pure that even his last breath was not for himself, but for those he loved."

The hall remained silent, not out of emptiness, but because every heart was full.

Abhirami's heart clenched. She knew this story well, yet in Guruji's voice, it carried a weight she had never felt before.

Guruji's gaze softened as he continued, "It is said that their souls could not ascend, held back by their suffering. For years, they lingered in the realm of the unseen, their presence felt in the winds that whispered through the trees, in the silence that settled over the land at dusk. It was only when a distant descendant, through great acts of charity and prayers, sought to free them that they were finally able to move beyond."

The Power of Release

Abhirami's mind flickered to the rituals she had seen in her own family—the offering of rice and water, the prayers whispered to the departed, the lamps lit in remembrance. She had often wondered if these acts were merely tradition or if they truly held the power to unshackle a soul bound by attachment.

Guruji's voice was soft yet unwavering. "The Jains believe that karma is like a fine net—it clings to the soul, determining its course across lifetimes. But just as karma binds, it can also be dissolved. And sometimes, the living must assist the departed in severing their final ties."

Rohith raised a hesitant hand. "How?"

Guruji smiled, his gaze brimming with understanding. "Through prayers, through forgiveness, through acts of selfless service. By letting go of grief by releasing our own attachments, we allow them to move forward. In Jain tradition, the ritual of 'Shraddha' is not merely a remembrance—it is an act of liberation. When we pray for them, we are not only honouring them but helping them ascend beyond the realm of longing."

The Stillness Beyond

Aastha closed her eyes. She thought of those who had left her world—relatives whose voices still echoed in memories, whose absence still left an ache. She had always held onto them in sorrow, but what if she had been holding them back?

She exhaled slowly, feeling a shift within her.

Guruji's voice was a murmur now, almost like the wind itself. *"Nothing in this world is truly lost. Every soul is on its own journey, and one day, we all find our way home."*

The Modern Medium:

Guruji's voice softened, carrying the weight of centuries of inquiry, belief, and scepticism. "Throughout history," he began, "there have been those who claim to communicate with spirits—mediums, psychics, spiritualists. Some, unfortunately, are mere charlatans, weaving illusions to prey on the vulnerable, turning grief into profit. But there are others… those who walk a different path, those who have seen beyond the veil, who have spoken words they could not have otherwise known, who have carried messages from realms beyond our perception."

Echoes from the Beyond

Guruji's eyes swept across the seekers before him. "There are stories," he said, "stories that challenge the very fabric of what we believe to be reality.

There is the tale of a child, barely four years old, who spoke in a dialect long lost to time. When questioned, he recalled vivid details of a life centuries past—names, places, and events that history itself had forgotten. Sceptics dismissed it as imagination, but when scholars traced his words, they found accounts eerily matching his descriptions."

Guruji continued, "There are those who, upon waking from near-death experiences, return with the knowledge they had never encountered before—visions of luminous beings, landscapes untouched by earthly bounds, encounters with loved ones long departed. Science has tried to explain this—some call it the firing of a dying brain, hallucinations, fragments of the subconscious. And yet… how does one explain the man who, after being clinically dead for minutes, recounts a conversation his family had in the waiting room, word for word? Or the blind woman who, after a near-death experience, describes colours she had never seen in her waking life?"

Are We Ready to Listen?

Guruji leaned forward, his voice dropping to a near whisper, and in that silence, his words carried even more weight.

"The real question," he said, "is not whether communication with the departed is possible—but whether we are ready to listen."

Guruji said, "For if the soul is eternal, if consciousness does not end but merely transforms, then death is not silence—it is simply another language. And like any language, it requires patience, openness, and a willingness to hear beyond the noise of our own doubts."

Apeksha's heart pounded. Could it be? Had the departed ever spoken to her, but she had not recognised the language?

Guruji closed his eyes for a moment, then said, "Sometimes, the dead do not speak in words. They speak in a sudden scent that reminds you of them. In a dream that feels too vivid to be mere imagination. In a song that plays at just the right moment, carrying a message only your heart can understand."

Silence fell over the hall again—not the silence of emptiness, but the silence of something vast and unseen.

And in that silence, Apeksha understood.

The veil between worlds was thinner than she had ever imagined.

Guruji, after a long and reflective pause, gently raised his hand, signalling for a short break. The devotees, still absorbed in the morning's profound discourse, rose slowly as though reluctant to part from the sacred energy that had enveloped them. They moved toward the refreshment counter, their footsteps unhurried, their hearts still echoing with the wisdom shared.

The air carried the inviting aroma of freshly brewed chai and fragrant herbal infusions, mingling with the soft rustle of leaves swaying in the gentle breeze. The sky stretched vast and unblemished, a tranquil shade of blue that seemed to mirror the stillness within the seekers' minds. Sunlight streamed through the canopy of ancient trees, dappling the ashram grounds in golden patterns, as though nature itself had conspired to create a perfect moment of reflection.

Some devotees strolled along the winding garden paths, their voices hushed, speaking in reverent tones as they unravelled the layers of Guruji's teachings. Others found quiet corners beneath the shade of banyan and peepul trees, sipping their warm beverages in silent contemplation, their thoughts drifting between the realms of the spoken and the unspoken. The entire ashram seemed to hum with an unspoken harmony, as if each leaf, each gust of wind, and each lingering word had become part of an intricate, sacred rhythm.

Aastha sat in deep discussion with Abhirami and Kiran, their voices animated yet measured, dissecting the nuances of the morning's wisdom. Their eyes shone with wonder, their minds yearning to grasp the depths of the mysteries unfurling before them.

When the devotees returned to the Buddha Hall, a palpable sense of anticipation filled the air. The soft golden light filtering through the high windows bathed the space in an almost ethereal glow, as if the very walls held the echoes of ancient truths waiting to be whispered once more. They took their seats with quiet reverence, their hearts open, their minds sharpened by curiosity and devotion.

The silence that followed was profound, yet it did not feel empty. It was the silence of deep listening, of souls attuned to something beyond words. Here, in this sacred space, they waited—not just to hear, but to receive. For they knew that in Guruji's next words lay another gateway to the boundless mysteries of existence, waiting to unfold in the light of timeless wisdom.

SECTION ONE

Evidence and Experiences

"The deepest experiences are not those we can measure with science, but those we feel in the heart—where the unseen world speaks to us, whispering of truths too vast for the mind to grasp."

- *Shree Shambav*

CHAPTER 1

Communicating with the Departed

"In the stillness of the soul, the departed speak not through words, but through signs, dreams, and subtle whispers, teaching us that the bond of love transcends the boundaries of life and death."

– Shree Shambav

Synopsis

This chapter explores the fascinating world of communication with the departed, focusing on how mediums, psychics, and spiritual practitioners claim to establish contact with souls who have passed on. It investigates the various methods employed, such as clairvoyance, channelling, and trance states, to facilitate these interactions. The chapter also critically examines the validity of such claims by looking at real-world examples, scientific studies, and anecdotal evidence to understand whether there is any measurable truth to these experiences. Questions surrounding the reliability of mediumship are addressed, considering how personal belief or scepticism can influence both the practice and interpretation of spirit communication. Additionally, the chapter delves into the role cultural and religious backgrounds play in shaping the acceptance or rejection of these practices, offering insights into the differing views on mediumship across the world. Through these lenses, the chapter seeks to provide a balanced perspective on the phenomenon of communicating with the departed while acknowledging the mysteries and complexities surrounding it.

Lalitha's voice carried both curiosity and scepticism as she asked, "Guruji, what methods do mediums and psychics use to claim communication with souls who have passed on?"

Guruji smiled gently. "Since the dawn of human consciousness," he began, "we have sought to understand what lies beyond the final breath. When a loved one departs, we ache for a sign, a whisper, a fleeting touch of their presence. This longing has given birth to those who claim to be messengers between worlds—mediums, psychics, shamans, and mystics. But how do they bridge the realms of the seen and the unseen?"

The Mirror Between Worlds: Methods of Spirit Communication

Guruji continued, his voice weaving stories into wisdom. "There is no single path, no universal key to the door of the beyond. Different traditions, different souls, have sought different ways."

The Art of Trance: Becoming an Empty Vessel

Guruji's voice carried the weight of ancient wisdom as he spoke. "To receive a message from beyond, one must first become empty—like a flute that only sings when the wind moves through it. Some mediums achieve this emptiness by entering a deep trance, allowing their own consciousness to step aside so that another presence may enter."

He paused, letting the silence settle before continuing.

"In ancient Greece, the great Oracle of Delphi sat upon a sacred tripod above a chasm, inhaling vapours that rose from the earth. She would fall into a trance, her body trembling, her voice speaking in cryptic tongues. Kings and philosophers travelled vast distances to seek her guidance, believing that Apollo himself spoke through her."

A hush fell over the hall as the seekers imagined the sacred temple, the flickering torches, the Oracle swaying as divine words passed through her lips.

"But trance-like states are not confined to the West," Guruji continued. "In **Vodou**, spirit possession is seen as a sacred act, where the body of the medium becomes a vessel for the Loa—powerful spirits who descend to communicate with the living. Their movements change, their voices shift, and those watching can feel an energy far beyond the physical."

Lalitha leaned forward, intrigued. "Guruji, how is this possible?"

Guruji's smile was knowing. "Think of it like this—when you dream, do you control the images that appear? Or do they come unbidden, as if whispered by some unseen hand? In the same way, a medium surrenders, allowing something beyond themselves to flow through."

He then spoke of modern trance mediums, those who claim to channel messages from the dead or beings from other dimensions. Some enter a hypnotic state, their voices shifting, their mannerisms changing as if another presence has stepped into their being. Others scribble words in frantic handwriting, messages they insist are not their own.

"But tell me," Guruji asked, his gaze piercing yet kind, "can a cup that is already full receive new water?"

The seekers pondered his words.

"A mind cluttered with doubt, fear, or ego may never hear the whispers from the other side," he said. "Only when we become empty, still as a silent lake, can we reflect the sky above and listen to the unseen?"

His words lingered in the air, like an unspoken invitation to those willing to open their hearts to mystery.

The Séance: A Circle of Intent

Guruji's voice deepened, carrying the weight of centuries-old mystery.

Lalitha felt a shiver travel down her spine.

"This," Guruji continued, "is the ancient ritual of the séance, a practice that has captivated and unsettled humanity for generations. It flourished in the Spiritualist movement of the 19th century, when people, consumed by the grief of lost loved ones, turned to mediums for solace. Some séances were later revealed as clever illusions—hidden wires, trick tables, assistants lurking in the shadows. But then… there were those moments, unexplainable, impossible to dismiss."

He paused, letting the weight of uncertainty settle upon his listeners.

"Even Sir Arthur Conan Doyle, the great creator of Sherlock Holmes, was a devoted believer in spirit communication. And then there was Thomas Edison, the mastermind behind the phonograph and the electric light. Did you know that he once considered building a *'Necrophone'* or *'spirit phone'*—a device designed to allow the departed to communicate through electrical frequencies?"

A ripple of astonishment passed through the room.

"Edison reasoned that if energy never truly disappears, then the essence of consciousness—of life itself—might continue in some form. And if souls persisted beyond death, might they not, too, manipulate electrical currents to speak?"

Guruji's gaze swept across the hall, searching their expressions.

"Does that sound so strange?" he asked. "Even now, scientists measure forces beyond our perception—radio waves, invisible yet carrying voices across the world; quantum entanglement, where two particles mirror each other's actions despite vast distances. We accept these things because they can be measured."

A hush fell over the hall as the weight of his words settled.

"But tell me," Guruji said, his voice dropping to a near whisper, "what if the voices of the departed travel on frequencies just beyond human perception? What if the whispers we dismiss as mere imagination are, in truth, echoes from another realm?"

Automatic Writing: Messages Through the Hand

"There is a method," Guruji said, "where the hand moves as if possessed by an unseen force—automatic writing. Here, the words do not come from conscious thought, nor are they shaped by logic or intent. Instead, they flow from a place beyond the known self, as though the hand becomes a vessel for a voice that seeks to be heard."

The devotees leaned in; their curiosity ignited.

"In ancient times," Guruji continued, "oracles and scribes claimed their hands were guided by divine forces. The Dead Sea Scrolls, for instance, contain texts believed to have been transcribed under prophetic inspiration. In China, Taoist shamans practised Fu Ji, where spirits were said to guide a suspended brush over sand or rice paper, forming intricate symbols that revealed sacred messages."

He paused, eyes gleaming with a deeper knowing.

Guruji let the silence stretch, allowing the weight of the mystery to sink in.

The Realm Between Worlds: When the Soul is Most Receptive

Guruji, after a pause, said, "But the simplest and most ancient way," he continued, "is through dreams and visions. When we sleep, the walls of the conscious mind fall away. The logical, reasoning self steps aside, and in that sacred space, souls slip through—whispering messages, appearing in forms that comfort or guide."

Lalitha's mind stirred with memory. She had dreamt of her grandmother many times—so vividly that she could feel the warmth of her embrace, hear the exact cadence of her voice. In those dreams, her grandmother would sit beside her on the old wooden swing, just as she had in childhood, offering advice with knowing eyes. Was it merely the mind clinging to the past? Or was it something more?

"In the Bible," Guruji continued, "angels appeared to prophets in dreams. Joseph, the earthly father of Jesus, was warned by an angel in a dream to flee to Egypt, saving the infant Christ from Herod's wrath. The entire course of history shifted because of a vision delivered in sleep."

The room was silent yet alive with thought.

"In Buddhism," Guruji said, "it is believed that enlightened masters visit their disciples in dreams, imparting wisdom when the mind is most open. There is a story of a devoted monk who longed to see the Buddha but lived centuries after his time. One night, in deep meditation, he saw the Tathagata in a vision. The Buddha spoke no words, yet in that silent presence, the monk received enlightenment. When he awoke, his doubts had vanished—his soul had been touched beyond what waking reality could offer."

Lalitha shivered.

"And in Sufism," Guruji continued, "there are countless stories of saints and mystics who guide their disciples through the realm of dreams. Jalaluddin Rumi, the great Sufi poet, once said:

'This place is a dream. Only a sleeper considers it real. Then death comes like dawn, and you wake up laughing at what you thought was your grief.'

Many seekers, lost in despair, have dreamt of their spiritual masters—felt their hands on their forehead, heard them whisper divine wisdom into their hearts. And upon waking, they knew with certainty: they had not been alone."

Lalitha felt the weight of his words settle deep within her. How often had she ignored the messages hidden in her own dreams? How often had she dismissed them as mere imagination when, perhaps, they were something far more profound?

Guruji's gaze softened as he looked at her. "Even now, if you close your eyes and listen—not with your ears, but with your soul—who knows what you might hear?"

She inhaled deeply. The world felt larger now, more mysterious, as though unseen hands gently nudged her toward an answer she had always known but had never dared to trust.

The True Question: Are We Willing to Listen?

A hush had fallen over the hall. The seekers sat in deep contemplation.

Guruji leaned forward, his voice no louder than a breath.

"But, my dear ones, the question is not merely how spirits communicate. The true question is: Are we willing to listen?"

The Veil Between Worlds: Science and the Unseen

John asked, "Guruji, how can the validity of mediumship and psychic abilities be evaluated through real-world examples or scientific studies?"

John's question hung in the air, a challenge wrapped in curiosity. He was a seeker, yet his mind craved evidence. Guruji acknowledged him with a serene nod before speaking. "This question," Guruji said, "is as old as human history itself. Can the unseen truly be measured? Can the whisper of a soul be weighed, the presence of the departed recorded in a ledger? Sceptics demand proof, while believers trust experience. And somewhere between the two, the truth waits—silent, unshaken."

"Science, with all its brilliance, has ventured into this mystery," he continued. "There have been studies, experiments, and cases that defy explanation. Let me tell you of one such attempt."

The Weight of a Soul

"In the early 20th century, Dr. Duncan MacDougall, a physician from Massachusetts, sought to measure the soul itself. He carefully placed dying patients on a precision scale, recording their weight before and after death. Time and again, at the exact moment of passing, there was a loss—21 grams.

Sceptics dismissed it as bodily fluids, but MacDougall was convinced. He believed he had measured the departure of the soul. The idea became a legend, inspiring debates and even films. Was it proof? Or merely a glimpse through a keyhole, hinting at something greater?"

John listened intently…

Messages from the Departed: The Psychic Who Knew Too Much

"Consider this," Guruji continued. "In the 20th century, there was a renowned medium named Leonora Piper. Her abilities were so astounding that she was investigated by the Society for Psychical Research, an organisation that sought to separate fraud from truth.

Researchers conducted rigorous tests, sending strangers to her with false identities. Yet, time and again, she revealed names, events, and secrets that no one but the departed could have known. Scientists—some sceptics themselves—had no explanation. William James, the father of American psychology, famously said that her abilities 'broke through his hardened materialism like a sunburst.'"

John shifted in his seat.

Visions of the Beyond: Near-Death Experiences

"But perhaps the most compelling evidence," Guruji said, "comes from those who have stood at the threshold of life and death itself—near-death experiences.

There are countless cases of people who have been clinically dead, their hearts silent, their brains devoid of activity. Yet when they return, they speak of things they could not possibly have seen.

A man in surgery, under total anaesthesia, later describes the exact moment a nurse dropped an instrument. A blind woman who has never seen light in her entire life returns from cardiac arrest, describing the faces of her doctors.

What do we make of this?" Guruji's voice was gentle but firm. "Science documents the phenomenon but struggles to explain it. Some say it is merely the mind grasping for meaning in its final moments. Others say it is proof—proof that consciousness is not bound to the body, that we exist beyond this flesh and bone."

The Candle and the Wind

John exhaled slowly, absorbing the weight of Guruji's words. He had come seeking certainty, but he was beginning to understand that truth was not always a line—it was a horizon, ever receding as one approached.

Guruji smiled knowingly. "Imagine a candle in a room. The flame flickers, dances, illuminates. That is the mind, the self. Now, imagine a wind blows, and the candle goes out. The flame disappears—but does it cease to exist? Or does it merely become part of something larger, unseen but present?"

The room was silent.

"Science may measure the candle," Guruji said. "But it is the soul that feels the wind."

John closed his eyes for a moment. He had come seeking proof. Instead, he had found something deeper—the realisation that some truths must be experienced, not explained.

The Lens of Perception: Belief, Skepticism, and the Unseen

Dev asked, "Guruji, what role does belief or scepticism play in the effectiveness or interpretation of spirit communication?"

Dev's question hung in the air like a bridge between two worlds—one of faith, one of doubt. The room was silent, each seeker waiting for Guruji's response.

Guruji smiled, his eyes reflecting both wisdom and patience. "Dev," he said gently, "imagine standing before a vast and infinite ocean. Some see only the waves, the restless movement on the surface. Others sense the depth beneath, unseen but undeniable. And then, there are those who refuse to believe the ocean exists at all—because they have only known the shore."

The Power of Belief: The Key to the Invisible

"Belief," Guruji continued, "is like a door. It does not create what lies beyond, but it determines whether one can step through. Across cultures, faith has been the force that allows people to perceive what others dismiss.

Think of the ancient oracles, the seers who spoke of things unseen. To those who believed, their words were revelations. To sceptics, they were mere coincidence or trickery. The same message, the same voice—yet two different realities."

He paused, then added, "Many who claim to have spoken with the departed say the spirits themselves are drawn to belief. It is not that doubt is wrong, but rather that an utterly closed mind becomes like a locked room—no light may enter, no whispers may be heard."

The Skeptic's Blind Spot: The Unseen Wind

Dev nodded, but there was still hesitation in his eyes. Guruji noticed and leaned forward slightly, his tone shifting. "Skepticism is necessary," he admitted. "It protects us from deception. There are frauds who prey upon the grieving, weaving illusions for profit. But extreme scepticism is like standing in a storm and denying the wind exists simply because you cannot see it."

He then told a story.

"There was once a scientist, a man of great intellect, who refused to believe in anything beyond the material world. One night, he had a dream—a vivid, overwhelming vision of his late mother speaking to him, guiding him. When he woke, he dismissed it as nothing more than his subconscious.

But days later, he received a letter in the mail—a message she had written before her passing, containing the very same words from his dream.

Was it a coincidence? Or had his scepticism blinded him to a truth too vast for logic alone?"

Faith and Fear: Two Sides of the Same Coin

"Dev," Guruji continued, "have you ever noticed that those who fear the dark are often those who do not believe in ghosts? Why should they fear what they claim does not exist?"

The question lingered.

"Doubt, you see, is not always born of reason—it is often the child of fear. The fear that if the unseen is real, then our understanding of reality must change.

That we are not alone. That there is more beyond what we can measure."

Dev swallowed as if something within him had shifted.

The Middle Path: The Open Mind

Guruji smiled. "The wise do not cling blindly to belief, nor do they barricade themselves behind scepticism. They walk the middle path—with an open heart and an inquiring mind.

It is like looking at the night sky. A believer sees a cosmic dance of the soul's ancestors watching over us. A sceptic sees only distant burning stars.

Who is right?"

"Perhaps both. Perhaps neither.

The real question, Dev, is not whether spirits speak.

It is whether we are truly listening."

Dev bowed his head, and in that moment, the question he had asked was no longer the question he carried.

The Veil of Belief: Culture, Faith, and the Unseen

Espen asked, "Guruji, how do cultural and religious views influence the acceptance or rejection of mediumship practices?"

Guruji gazed at him with quiet contemplation before speaking. "Espen," he said, "imagine a traveller who walks through many lands, each with its own sky, its own customs, its own understanding of the world. Though the same sun shines upon all, each culture sees its light through a different lens. The same is true for how people view the unseen—the voices beyond the veil, the whispers of spirits."

He shifted slightly in his seat. "Some traditions embrace the invisible, seeing it as a bridge between the realms. Others fear it, branding it as deception or even darkness. And some simply close their eyes to it, convinced that what cannot be measured cannot exist."

The Embrace of the Mystical: Cultures That Welcome the Unseen

"In many Indigenous traditions," Guruji continued, "the line between the living and the dead is not a boundary, but a doorway. The ancestors walk beside their descendants, whispering guidance through dreams, signs, and the voices of shamans. In these cultures, mediumship is not an anomaly—it is expected. A gift passed through generations, nurtured like a sacred flame.

Look at Shinto in Japan—where spirits, or kami, inhabit all things. The departed do not vanish; they linger in nature, in the wind that rustles through ancient trees, in the warmth of a hearth, in the presence felt but unseen. Mediums, in this belief, do not summon spirits—they merely listen."

He paused, his eyes sweeping across the room, before continuing.

"And then, there are those who seek the unseen not with blind reverence but with measured caution. In many African and Afro-Caribbean spiritual traditions—Vodou, Santería, and Candomblé—communication with spirits is both a sacred gift and a formidable responsibility. The spirits may offer guidance, but they may also test, deceive, or demand something in return. The role of the medium is not merely to hear—but to discern, to navigate the unseen with wisdom, knowing whom to trust and when to walk away."

Guruji's voice carried the weight of ancient wisdom as he continued.

"These traditions, often misunderstood by the outside world, trace their origins to the spiritual heritage of the Yoruba people of West Africa. They are sister faiths, sharing a deep reverence for the divine forces that govern existence. In Vodou, practised predominantly in Haiti, these spirits are known as Loa—powerful intermediaries between the human and divine. In Santería, rooted in Cuba, they are the Orishas, celestial beings who guide and protect. In Candomblé, flourishing in Brazil, the same Orishas are worshipped through ritual dance, music, and trance.

But in all three traditions, there is an unshakable truth: not all spirits who answer the call come with benevolent intent. That is why rituals of protection, offerings, and ancestral veneration are vital—acts not just of devotion, but of spiritual safeguarding."

Guruji paused, his gaze sweeping across the room.

"So, the question is not simply whether spirits can communicate. It is—how do we know which voices to trust?"

The Fear of the Unseen: When the Door Must Remain Closed

Guruji's expression grew sombre. "But in some cultures," he said, "to speak with spirits is to invite danger. To seek the dead is to tamper with forces best left undisturbed."

His voice softened.

"In Christianity, the Bible speaks of prophets receiving visions, of angels descending with divine messages. Yet, it also warns against necromancy—against calling upon the dead for knowledge. This is why, in many Christian traditions, mediumship is seen as something to be wary of. Is it the voice of a spirit? Or something darker, masquerading as light?"

Guruji let the question linger before continuing.

"In Islam, too, the unseen is acknowledged—jinn, spirits, and the souls of the departed exist beyond our perception. Yet, seeking them out is discouraged, for what walks in shadow may not always be what it seems."

He sighed gently. "And then, there are the cultures shaped by modern science—where the unseen is often dismissed altogether. In these places, spirits are folklore, and mediums are either entertainers or deceivers. The world, to them, is only what can be measured, tested, and proven."

The Story of the Blind Men and the Elephant: Many Truths, One Reality

Guruji folded his hands and smiled. "There is an ancient story," he said, "of blind men who were led to an elephant. Each touched a different part—one felt the trunk and declared that an elephant was like a snake. Another touched the leg and insisted it was like a tree. A third, feeling the ear, believed it to be like a great fan.

They argued, each certain that he alone knew the truth.

But none had seen the whole."

He looked at Espen. "So it is with the unseen. Each culture, each faith, and each sceptic sees only a part of the great mystery. Some embrace it, some fear it, some deny it. But in the end, the elephant remains, whether one believes in it or not."

Guruji's gaze softened. "The question is not whether mediumship is real. That is a question bound by belief, shaped by culture, coloured by tradition."

The real question is—if the voices of the departed do call out, how many are willing to listen? And how many turn away simply because their world has not made space for such things?"

The room was silent. Espen, lost in thought, slowly bowed his head in gratitude.

Guruji, after a long and reflective pause. His voice, gentle yet firm, carried through the tranquil air.

"Let us break for the midday meal."

The devotees slowly rose from their seats, still wrapped in the lingering echoes of the morning's discourse. They walked in measured steps from the Buddha Hall to the food canteen, their minds oscillating between contemplation and conversation. The scent of freshly prepared food filled the air—

steaming rice, fragrant dal, and warm chapatis served with love and simplicity. The rhythmic clinking of utensils blended seamlessly with the gentle murmur of voices, forming a symphony of quiet gratitude.

After the meal, some devotees retreated to their shelters for rest, while others returned to the Buddha Hall, drawn by the stillness it offered. A few wandered into the ashram gardens, their feet finding the cool earth as they strolled beneath the shade of ancient trees.

Under the large banyan tree—their usual meeting place—Akshaya, Rohith, and Vasudeva gathered, their companionship a familiar rhythm in the vastness of the retreat. Soon, Nita, Lalitha, Sujitha, and Espen joined them, followed by Astyn and Kieron, their presence adding warmth to the circle. Bhavya, Aarna, and Dev were deeply engrossed in discussing the morning session, their words charged with insight and curiosity. The others listened in quiet reverence, absorbing the wisdom exchanged between them.

Vidyarthi, who had been listening intently, turned to Sam, his expression contemplative.

"Sam, I've seen you in many retreats," he said thoughtfully. "You have been here for a long time. Everyone has their story—what brought them here, what they seek. I have always wondered about yours.

Of course, I don't mean to compel you, but… I felt I should ask."

Before Sam could respond, Sofia, her voice gentle yet curious, leaned in.

"Sam, does it bother you to share?"

Sam exhaled slowly as though releasing a weight he had long carried. A small, fleeting smile touched his lips before he finally spoke.

"Not actually… but… alright."

A hush settled over the group as Sam began his story.

"I am an orphan," he said, his voice steady but tinged with the echoes of a past filled with longing. "I have never seen my parents. I spent my entire childhood in a Christian missionary orphanage. The man who took care of me—Father Francis—was the closest thing I had to family. For me, he was more than a guardian. He was my shelter when I was lost, my light in the dark."

His gaze drifted into the distance as if looking through the veil of time.

"I asked him countless times—why did my parents leave me here? Were they still alive? Did they ever think of me?"

Sam's voice softened. "Each time, Father Francis would give me the same answer:

'There is a reason for everything, my son. Have faith in the Divine.'"

Life went on. Sam buried himself in studies and found solace in music. He excelled in academics, earning scholarships that placed him in prestigious institutions. With every achievement, he felt he was justifying his existence—proving, perhaps to himself, that he was worthy of the life he had been given.

"In business school, I met Amelia," he continued, his voice carrying a note of warmth. "She was brilliant—smart, kind-hearted, full of life. We became friends, and over the years, that friendship grew into something deeper. She understood me in a way no one ever had."

A small smile played on his lips as he recalled those days.

"We both secured jobs at top MNCs, earning more than we had ever imagined. Yet, despite our busy schedules, we made time for something we both cared deeply about—helping underprivileged children. Every weekend, we volunteered, giving free lessons, offering guidance… It became the most fulfilling part of our lives."

His expression turned tender.

"One day, I proposed to her. She accepted, and we married in the presence of Father Francis, who, by then, had grown old and fragile. I told Amelia that he was not just a priest to me—he was my father, my mother, my divine."

Sam paused, his eyes glistening with emotion. "Hearing this, Father Francis wept. He embraced me and said,

'Son, you are a noble soul. Be sure in what you do, but never let the current of life make you forget the people who matter. Moments, once lost, never return.'"

A heavy silence followed, each word sinking into the hearts of those listening.

"Not long after, Father Francis passed away," Sam continued, his voice quieter now. "The man who had been my pillar, my guide, was no more. I had his memories, but memories, no matter how vivid, cannot replace presence."

He exhaled deeply as though shedding an invisible burden.

"Life moved forward. I decided to quit my corporate job and start my own business—a dream I had carried for years. But Amelia… she wasn't happy with my decision."

Sam's voice wavered slightly.

"She said, 'Sam, we already have so little time together. If you start a business, we'll have even less. Why do we need more than what God has already given us?'"

His words lingered in the air, heavy with unspoken emotions.

Just then, Kiran sighed, checking the time. "The session is about to begin."

One by one, the devotees rose, their minds still entangled in the depth of Sam's story. They began their quiet walk back to the Buddha Hall, where Guruji's next words awaited—words that might offer new perspectives, new answers, or perhaps new questions to ponder.

Sam lingered for a moment beneath the banyan tree, feeling the presence of unseen hands guiding him forward.

For some questions, he realised, the answers did not come immediately. They revealed themselves in time, in moments, in choices yet to unfold.

.

CHAPTER II

Is Reincarnation Real? Evidence and Insights

"The evidence of reincarnation is not always found in facts, but in the echoes of memories that stir deep within us—whispers of lives we've lived and the souls we've known, beyond the veils of time."

- Shree Shambav

Synopsis

The chapter investigates the concept of reincarnation, drawing on case studies of children who have recalled memories of past lives, cultural beliefs, and spiritual teachings that support the idea of the soul's continuous journey across lifetimes. It explores how reincarnation is understood in different spiritual and cultural contexts, examining the various interpretations of life, death, and rebirth around the world. The chapter also delves into the role of consciousness in this cycle, discussing how the soul evolves through experiences across multiple lifetimes, with an emphasis on the karmic learning process that shapes each new incarnation. Additionally, it addresses the scientific and sceptical challenges to reincarnation, presenting the arguments against its validity and exploring the responses from those who believe in the phenomenon. Through a blend of case studies, philosophical reflections, and cultural analysis, this chapter offers a comprehensive look at the evidence and insights surrounding reincarnation.

Is Reincarnation Real? Evidence and Insights.

The afternoon light streamed through the high windows of the Buddha Hall, casting long shadows on the polished floor. The air was thick with contemplation, the silence carrying the weight of unspoken questions.

Sofia hesitated for a moment before speaking.

"Guruji," she said, her voice carrying a mixture of curiosity and reverence, "Is reincarnation real?"

A soft smile crossed Guruji's face. "Sofia," he said gently, "this question is as old as humanity itself. It is not merely a matter of belief, but of experience—of what the soul remembers when the body forgets."

The room was utterly still.

"Throughout history, there have been those who recall lives they have never lived—children who speak of places they have never been, of families they have never met. In the scriptures of many traditions, reincarnation is not a fantasy but a profound truth, a rhythm as natural as the rising and setting of the sun."

He paused, letting the words settle before continuing.

The Memories of Children: Evidence from the Present

"There was a boy in India," Guruji began, his voice filled with quiet intensity, "who, at the age of three, began speaking of a past life. He recalled the name of a village miles away, the house he had lived in, and even the way he had died. His family, sceptical at first, eventually travelled to the village. To their astonishment, the details matched. The boy recognised his 'past-life' family and even pointed out where he had hidden money before his previous death."

He looked around the hall, noting the expressions of intrigue.

"This is not an isolated case. Dr. Ian Stevenson, a psychiatrist who spent decades researching past-life memories, documented over 2,500 cases of children who recalled previous lives. Many of them spoke languages they had never learned, described places they had never seen, and recognised people they had never met."

Ancient Wisdom: Reincarnation Across Traditions

Guruji's gaze softened.

"But this is not a discovery of modern science alone. The idea of reincarnation is woven into the very fabric of ancient wisdom."

He turned to Sofia.

"In the Bhagavad Gita Chapter 2, Verse 22, Lord Krishna tells Arjuna:

Just as a person discards worn-out clothes and puts on new ones, so too does the soul abandon old bodies and enter new ones."

Guruji let the words sink in before continuing.

"In Buddhism, the cycle of birth, death, and rebirth—**Samsara**—is a fundamental truth. The Dalai Lama himself is chosen based on the past-life memories of a child who recalls hidden objects and previous connections."

His voice dropped to a near whisper.

"In the Gospels, when Jesus' disciples ask about the return of Elijah, he responds:

'And if you are willing to accept it, he is the Elijah who was to come.' (Matthew 11:14)

This passage has long intrigued scholars and spiritual seekers alike. In Jewish tradition, Elijah was believed to return before the coming of the Messiah. Yet, Jesus identifies John the Baptist as Elijah—not in the literal sense, but as the continuation of his prophetic mission.

Does this not suggest the idea of a soul returning in a new form, carrying forward an unfinished purpose? While Christian doctrine does not explicitly endorse reincarnation, this verse, along with others, hints at a deeper mystery—that souls may transcend individual lifetimes, fulfilling divine roles across ages, much like a river that disappears into the earth, only to resurface elsewhere, flowing ever onward."

Sofia's eyes widened slightly.

Guruji continued, "The Sufis speak of the soul as a traveller, moving through lifetimes as a river flows through different lands, always seeking the ocean of the Divine. Rumi, the great Sufi mystic, once wrote:

"I died as mineral and became a plant,

I died as plant and rose to animal,

I died as animal and I was human,

Why should I fear? When was I less by dying?

Yet once more I shall die human,

To soar with angels blessed above."

He paused, his expression serene.

"In Zen Buddhism, there is a profound koan that asks: *'What was your original face before you were born?'* This is not merely a riddle but a gateway to deeper understanding. It challenges us to look beyond the illusion of individuality and time, beyond the fleeting identity of a single lifetime.

Zen teaches that our existence is not confined to this body or this moment. Just as a wave is not separate from the ocean, our essence flows through different forms beyond birth and death. Who we truly are is not bound by a single lifetime but is part of the infinite unfolding of existence."

The Soul's Journey: An Analogy

Guruji leaned forward slightly, his tone gentle yet profound.

"Imagine a candle," he said. "When it burns out, another candle is lit from its flame. Is it the same flame or a different one?"

The room was silent.

"This is reincarnation," he continued. "The body perishes, but consciousness—like the flame—continues, igniting a new life. The essence remains, though the form changes."

He looked toward the banyan tree outside the window, its gnarled roots deep in the earth.

"In Taoism, the journey of the soul is like a tree shedding its leaves in autumn, knowing that new ones will bloom in spring. The tree does not mourn its fallen leaves, nor does it resist the seasons. It simply allows life to flow."

The Question That Remains

Guruji turned back to Sofia.

"The real question is not whether reincarnation is real," he said, his voice barely above a whisper. "The real question is—if it is true, what does it mean for you?"

Sofia sat still, her mind racing, yet deeply calm.

"If you have lived before," Guruji continued, "what lessons have you carried into this life? What patterns repeat? What unfinished threads must you weave into completion?"

His eyes gleamed with kindness.

"Reincarnation is not merely about remembering the past," he said. "It is about understanding the present and shaping the future."

The devotees sat in profound stillness, their hearts expanding with the weight of this realisation.

Somewhere in the distance, a bird called out—a voice from another time, another life, echoing across the infinite river of existence.

Astyn asked, "Guruji, what evidence exists to support reincarnation, such as documented cases of children recalling past lives?"

Guruji closed his eyes for a moment as if gathering the weight of centuries before he spoke. "Reincarnation is not merely a belief," he began. "It is a mystery woven into the very fabric of existence, whispered through time, recorded in sacred texts, and witnessed in the lives of those who remember—those whose souls refuse to be bound by a single name, a single body."

The devotees leaned in, drawn by the magnetic pull of his words.

The Child Who Remembered a Life Left Behind

"In a small village in India," Guruji continued, "there was a boy named Shyam. From the time he could speak, he spoke not of toys and fairy tales but of another home, another family. He would cry in the night, not for his mother, but for another woman— one he called 'Ma' in a dialect unfamiliar to his village. He would insist that he had been a merchant in a city far away, that he had been murdered, and that his real name was Ravi."

The villagers dismissed it as a child's imagination—until he described, with alarming precision, the layout of a house in a town he had never visited. He recalled the names of people, the landmarks of a street unknown to him. When taken to that distant town, he walked straight to the home he had described, recognising faces and calling strangers by name.

"The most haunting detail?" Guruji's voice lowered. "He led the family to a place near the river and said, 'This is where my body was thrown.' And when they searched, they found records of a man named Ravi—who had indeed been murdered years before, just as the child had described."

A silence fell over the gathering, thick with the weight of the story.

The Western Scholar and the Repeating Soul

"This phenomenon is not confined to India," Guruji continued. "In the West, Dr. Ian Stevenson, a psychiatrist at the University of Virginia, spent decades studying such cases. He documented thousands of children who spoke of past lives with astonishing accuracy—children who bore birthmarks where they claimed to have suffered fatal wounds, children who spoke languages they had never learned."

One such case was James Leininger, a boy from Louisiana who, at just two years old, began describing vivid memories of being a World War II pilot. He would wake screaming from nightmares of crashing in a fiery explosion. He spoke of aircraft mechanics with the precision of a veteran, named obscure military details no toddler could know, and even identified the name of a fellow soldier—who had indeed fought alongside a pilot who had perished in combat.

Was this simply a coincidence? Or was it proof that the soul carries echoes of its past?"

The Science of Remembering

"But can science explain this?" Astyn asked, his curiosity burning like a flame.

Guruji nodded. "Science approaches reincarnation cautiously, yet the evidence persists. Dr. Stevenson's work, and later studies by Dr. Jim Tucker, show that young children often recall past lives with the greatest clarity—before the memories fade around the age of six like mist dissolving in the morning sun. Some researchers believe that these memories could be stored in the subconscious, that the mind carries an imprint beyond physical birth."

He paused. "But I ask you this—must all truths be measured in laboratories to be real? Do you doubt the wind because you cannot see it, though you feel it against your skin? Do you question love because it cannot be bottled, though it moves mountains? Some things must be known not by the mind but by the soul."

The Choice of the Soul

"Perhaps the real question," Guruji said, his voice now a whisper of eternity, "is not whether reincarnation is real, but why it happens.

If we return, what lessons have we left unfinished? What bonds still hold us? Whose laughter still echoes in our hearts, calling us back?"

Astyn exhaled, his thoughts unravelling like silk threads, weaving together the fragments of faith, science, and memory.

The banyan tree above them swayed gently in the wind as if nodding in silent agreement—whispering its ancient wisdom, rooted in lifetimes unknown.

Aarna asked, "Guruji, how do spiritual teachings and cultural beliefs around reincarnation differ across the world?"

"Aarna," he said gently, "reincarnation is like a river—though it flows through different lands, though it is given different names, its essence remains the same. Some see it as a sacred cycle of learning, others as a divine test, and still others as an illusion to be transcended. But always, beneath it, there is the question: 'What happens after we die? And who, truly, are we?'"

The gathering grew silent, drawn into the gravity of his words.

Hinduism: The Eternal Journey of the Soul

"In the ancient wisdom of the Vedas and the Upanishads, reincarnation—Samsara—is a truth as old as existence itself. The soul is eternal, passing from one body to another, just as a traveller change garments. But this journey is not without purpose. Each birth is a lesson, a step toward Moksha—liberation from the cycle of death and rebirth."

"Karma," he said, "is not reward or punishment, nor is it fate written in stone. It is a law as natural as the cycle of the seasons, as the river flowing to the sea. Just as the seed of a banyan tree carries within it the potential for a mighty forest, so too do our actions carry the potential for our next birth."

He looked around at the seekers gathered beneath the great banyan tree, its roots twisting deep into the earth, its branches stretching toward the sky.

"Imagine a merchant," he said, "a man of great wealth, but his heart is hard. He hoards his riches, turning away the hungry, deaf to the cries of those in need.

When he dies, his wealth does not follow him. What remains is the emptiness he created in others, the suffering he ignored. And so, in his next life, he is born into poverty—not as punishment, but so that he may experience what he once turned away from, so that his soul may learn the lesson of generosity."

Guruji paused, letting the weight of the words settle.

"Now imagine another man—a simple farmer. He owns little but gives freely. He feeds the wandering monk, he shelters the traveller, and he shares his last grain of rice with a hungry child. His heart is rich, though his pockets are empty. When he leaves this world, his kindness does not die with him. It follows, like the fragrance of a flower lingering in the air even after the bloom has fallen. And so, in his next life, he is born into abundance—not as a reward, but because his soul has understood the lesson of giving, and now he must learn the lesson of responsibility."

A gentle breeze stirred the leaves above as if the universe itself whispered its agreement.

"But remember," Guruji continued, his voice low yet steady, "karma is not a simple equation. It is not merely 'good deeds equal good life' or 'bad deeds equal suffering.' It is deeper than that. It is the sculptor of the soul. A man who is selfish does not return as poor simply to suffer—he returns so that he may see life from another side, so that his heart may soften, so that he may choose differently. A kind man is not born into wealth as a mere prize—he is given new challenges, new tests, to see if his heart remains as open when surrounded by luxury."

He smiled, his eyes filled with compassion, "You see, karma is not a judge nor an executioner. It is a teacher. A river must return to the sea, just as the soul must return to its source. But how it flows, how it carves its path through the valleys of existence—that is determined by the choices we make."

The seekers sat in silence, absorbing the depth of his words, each reflecting on the unseen ripples of their past and the currents shaping their future.

Buddhism: The Wheel of Suffering

"But the Buddha," Guruji continued, "saw reincarnation differently. He did not deny it, but he asked: 'What is it that truly reincarnates?' If the self is an illusion, what is being reborn?"

He paused, letting the question settle like dust on an ancient path.

"Imagine," Guruji said, "a traveller wandering through a vast desert, searching endlessly for water. With every mirage he chases, he finds only sand slipping through his fingers. Thirsty, exhausted, he stumbles forward, unaware that he is bound to this endless journey by the very thirst that drives him."

He paused, letting the image settle in their minds.

"This is the cycle of Samsara—the wheel of birth, death, and rebirth. It is not the body that continues, but the longing, the hunger, the attachments we carry. Like a flame passed from one candle to another, life continues—not as the same identity, but as the same burning desire."

He gestured toward the towering banyan tree.

"Look at that tree. Once, it was a seed. The seed was not the tree, yet without the seed, the tree would not be. In the same way, your past self is not you, but you are shaped by its choices, just as your future self will be shaped by the choices you make now."

He then recited softly: (Dhammapada 127)

"Not in the sky, nor the depths of the sea,

nor in the deepest caves of the mountains—

there is nowhere one can escape

the consequences of one's deeds."

The words hung in the air like an eternal truth woven into the fabric of existence.

"In the Jataka tales, the Buddha speaks of his many past lives—sometimes as a prince, sometimes as a hermit, sometimes even as an animal. With each birth, he carried the remnants of his past choices, learning, growing, and moving ever closer to awakening. But most of us are not yet awake. We are caught in the dream of desire, pulled forward by craving, trapped in the illusion that we are separate from the whole."

"To be free," Guruji continued, "one must awaken. See the mirages for what they are. Let go of attachment, and the wheel of rebirth dissolves like mist in the morning sun."

Christianity: The Hidden Whispers of Rebirth

"But what of the West?" Aarna asked, leaning forward.

Guruji's eyes gleamed with an intensity that seemed to pierce through time itself. His voice, steady and deliberate, carried the weight of forgotten wisdom.

"Reincarnation is not absent in Christianity," he said. "It is simply veiled, hidden in whispers, in forgotten texts and cryptic verses. A truth is once spoken, then carefully buried beneath centuries of doctrine."

He looked at the gathering, his gaze lingering on each seeker as if inviting them to remember something they had long known but lost along the way.

He then quoted from the Gospels, Matthew 11:14:

"And if you are willing to accept it, he is the Elijah who was to come."

"Did Jesus not hint that John the Baptist was the returned soul of Elijah? That the great prophet had walked this earth once before, only to return with a new name, a new form? Was this not a quiet acknowledgement of the soul's journey beyond a single lifetime?"

Guruji continued, his voice now carrying the hush of ancient knowledge.

"The early Christian sects—the Gnostics—believed in the soul's journey through many lifetimes. They did not see existence as a single fleeting moment but as a grand unfolding, a path of learning and purification. One of Christianity's earliest scholars, Origen of Alexandria, a man of profound intellect and spiritual depth, wrote:

'The soul has neither beginning nor end… it passes from one world to another, taking on different forms according to its previous deeds.'

He paused, allowing the weight of his words to settle.

"Why?" Guruji finally asked, his voice soft but unwavering. "Perhaps because a man who believes in many lives does not fear hellfire—he believes in redemption, in learning, in second chances. He does not see himself as condemned but as evolving. A soul that has wandered that has made mistakes, but that always has the opportunity to return, to grow, to find its way back to the divine."

The wind whispered through the trees as if carrying the echoes of forgotten teachings.

"Imagine," Guruji said, "a sculptor chiselling away at a block of marble. With each strike, he shapes the stone, refining, carving, and correcting. If he makes a mistake, he does not abandon the marble—he continues, knowing that perfection is not immediate but revealed through patience. So, too, is the soul shaped across lifetimes. Each birth is another stroke of the chisel, each experience another refinement, until the rough stone becomes the divine masterpiece it was always meant to be."

Sufism: The Soul's Endless Dance

"In the poetry of Rumi, in the heart of Sufism, reincarnation is not a doctrine, but a love story—the soul's longing for the Divine. He sang:

'I died as mineral and became a plant,

I died as plant and rose to animal,

I died as animal and I was man.

Why should I fear? When was I less by dying?'

"Sufis do not argue over whether reincarnation is real or not. To them, life itself is an illusion. They see the soul as a lover dancing toward God, shedding forms like veils, until at last, it dissolves completely in the Beloved."

Taoism: The Flow of the Universe

Guruji's voice softened, taking on the measured stillness of a river flowing endlessly toward the sea.

"And in China," he continued, "the Taoists speak not of reincarnation in the way others do, but of the great Flow—Qi, the energy that moves through all things. To them, life and death are not beginnings or endings but shifting currents within the same eternal river. The drop of rain that falls into the ocean does not cease to exist—it becomes the wave, then the mist, then the storm, only to return again as rain. So too does the essence of life transform, never truly vanishing."

The wind stirred the trees, rustling the leaves as if whispering forgotten wisdom.

"In the Tao Te Ching," Guruji continued, "it is written:

To return to the root is to find peace. To flow with the Way is to be eternal.'

The Taoists do not cling to the notion of an individual soul being reborn in another body. Instead, they see existence as a vast, unfolding pattern where all things dissolve and reform without ever truly departing. The fish becomes the bird, the tree becomes the mountain, the breath of one man becomes the laughter of another."

He paused, letting the imagery settle in the minds of his listeners.

"There is a story," he said, "of Zhuangzi, the great Taoist sage. One night, he dreamt he was a butterfly, fluttering effortlessly on the wind, completely free. When he awoke, he was Zhuangzi again. But he wondered—was he a man who had dreamt he was a butterfly, or a butterfly now dreaming he was a man?"

The devotees listened, caught in the mystery of the tale.

"That is the way of the Tao," Guruji explained. "Not to grasp at the illusion of permanence, but to understand that we are all shifting forms within the great unfolding. The river does not lament becoming the sea. The leaf does not fear falling to the earth, for it knows it will become the soil that nourishes the tree. So, too, must we understand that what we call 'life' and 'death' are merely movements of the same great current. To resist this is to suffer. To flow with it is to find peace."

He gazed at the assembly, his eyes holding the depth of a thousand rivers.

"So tell me," he said, his voice barely above a whisper, "are you the one dreaming of eternity, or is eternity dreaming through you?"

He smiled. "So you see, Aarna, while the names change, the essence remains. Whether it is called reincarnation, Samsara, Qi, or the will of God, the lesson is the same:

We are not just this body.

We have been here before.

And we will be here again, until we awaken to who we truly are."

Aarna exhaled, feeling the weight of a thousand lives resting upon her shoulders.

Aastha asked, "Guruji, what are the implications of reincarnation for the evolution of consciousness and karmic learning?"

Guruji closed his eyes for a moment. "Aastha," he said gently, "imagine a sculptor working on a block of marble. With each strike of his chisel, he carves away imperfection, revealing a form hidden within. But the work is not completed in a single day—it takes years, lifetimes, an eternity, perhaps. Each incarnation is another strike of the chisel, another refinement of the soul's essence."

The devotees listened, their breath caught in the stillness of the moment.

"Reincarnation is not just the recycling of bodies," Guruji continued. "It is the evolution of consciousness itself. The soul is like a traveller, journeying through countless landscapes, each life offering lessons that shape its understanding. Some lives teach love, others lose. Some bring power, others humility. But through it all, there is learning, refinement—karma shaping destiny, like the river smoothing the jagged stone."

He glanced at the ancient banyan tree nearby, its gnarled roots weaving into the earth like stories interwoven across time.

"In the Bhagavad Gita, Krishna says:

Just as a man discards old clothes and wears new ones, so too does the soul discard old bodies and take on new ones.'

But why does this happen? Because the soul carries unfinished lessons, unfulfilled longings, and unresolved debts. Each birth is an opportunity—a continuation of a story written over lifetimes. A cruel king may return as a beggar to learn humility. A mother who grieves the loss of her child may be born as her own daughter's child, the bond unbroken by death.

The hand that strikes in one life may return in another to offer healing. Karma is not punishment—it is the universe's way of bringing balance."

Aastha's eyes brimmed with thought. "But Guruji, does that mean suffering is inevitable? Are we bound to this cycle forever?"

Guruji smiled, his expression serene. "No cycle lasts forever, my child. Like a wheel spinning in the mud, one must realise that struggle is not the way out—awakening is. The Buddha taught that we are caught in *samsara*, the cycle of birth and rebirth, because of attachment and ignorance. We chase desires, grasp at illusions, and in doing so, we return again and again. But when one sees clearly—when one understands the impermanence of all things, when one releases the self—then the wheel stops. Then, there is liberation."

His voice softened, and he spoke as if to the wind itself.

"In Sufism, they say the soul is a moth drawn to the flame of the Divine. It circles and circles, lifetime after lifetime, seeking, yearning. But when it finally surrenders, when it lets go of itself entirely, it merges into the light—it becomes the very fire it once sought."

The devotees sat in silence as if the very air around them had grown heavy with meaning.

"To understand reincarnation," Guruji concluded, "is to understand that we are not merely living—we are unfolding. We are sculptors and sculptors both, shaping ourselves with every choice, every thought, every act of love or cruelty. But the day will come when the work is finished, when the marble is no longer a rough stone but a masterpiece. That is when the soul rests. That is when it returns home."

Guruji said, "Let me share a tale of a prince named Siddharth, who grappled with a mysterious ailment, the final throes of life tightening their grip on him. Siddharth was the sole heir to the throne, his father being the esteemed King Aditya. Despite exhausting every conceivable remedy and summoning the most skilled physicians from every corner of his vast kingdom, Siddharth's health continued to deteriorate, and no medicine could offer him respite. After an exhaustive pursuit of a cure, it became painfully apparent that all that remained was to await the inevitable."

One of the physicians in the king's service spoke with a heavy heart, addressing the monarch, "Your Majesty, despite our unwavering efforts, we can only hope that his passing may come without prolonged suffering."

Upon hearing these words, the queen's tears flowed freely, and an air of profound emotion enveloped everyone in the presence of the anguished king.

The king inquired, "Physician, can you tell me how much time he has left?"

The physician initially hesitated, taking a moment before responding, "Your Majesty, he will not survive until sunrise; this night will be his last."

Upon hearing these words, the king was overcome with sorrow, yet he also consoled himself with the inevitability of death. Recognising the certainty of the situation, the king took a seat beside his ailing son, determined to stay awake throughout the entire night, keeping vigil by his side.

The king cherished the precious memories he had shared with his son, struggling to come to terms with the impending loss of his only child in the coming years. A whirlwind of thoughts and emotions swirled in his mind as the early hours of dawn drew nearer. Eventually, the weariness overcame him, and despite his inner turmoil, the king succumbed to sleep. In slumber, his worries and concerns dissolved, granting him a peaceful respite.

In the depths of slumber, the king was granted a wondrous dream. In this dream, he reigned as a powerful monarch, the ruler of the entire universe. His heart swelled with joy as he gazed upon his beautiful and healthy children, each radiating intelligence and beauty. Beside him stood his beloved, the epitome of kindness and grace. Their abode was a magnificent golden palace adorned with unimaginable wealth and precious jewels, symbols of his boundless prosperity.

His name echoed far and wide as he commanded the mightiest of armies and was beloved by every soul within his realm. On this day, a grand celebration engulfed the kingdom, and the air resonated with the joyous cheers of his subjects. The king and his family revelled in the festivities with unbridled exuberance.

Yet, amid his blissful reverie, as he dwelt deeply in the dream's embrace, his only son drew his final breath in the waking world. The piercing cry of the queen, echoing with profound loss and agony, shattered the tranquillity of the dream. The anguished wail reverberated in his slumbering ears, accompanied by the frantic footsteps of those who rushed to the scene.

The cacophony of grief and despair yanked the king from his idyllic reverie, tearing him away from the empire he had momentarily possessed. His golden palace vanished into thin air, and his beautiful children dissolved like mirages. The gentle, kind queen faded from his sight, and his abundance of treasure disappeared into the void. In an instant, the king's world crumbled before him, and he awoke to a reality where his son had departed, his queen mourned in agony, and his entire kingdom wept for the loss of their future ruler.

Amidst these tumultuous events, the king bore a serene countenance, his lips adorned with a gentle smile. Observing this peculiar display, the queen couldn't contain her bewilderment. She inquired, "What has come over you? Have you, my lord, turned impervious to sorrow? Is it possible that you don't grieve for the loss of our son? You appear so different now, even though our child has departed, you wear a smile."

In response, Aditya, with a contemplative look, said, "I find myself in a bewildering quandary, my love. Should my heart be heavy with grief for the son who now rests in eternal slumber, or should it swell with joy for the fleeting glimpse I had of our beautiful children just moments ago? Should I mourn the loss of an empire that stretched across the universe, an abundance of wealth, and the opulent splendour of a golden palace? Or should I celebrate the memory of a life where I commanded the mightiest of armies? In the blink of an eye, all I possessed dissolved into the void as soon as I opened my eyes."

Aditya's voice trembled with a deep well of emotion as he spoke, his words laden with profound reflection. "As I closed my eyes, the image of my son in his final moments did not even cross my mind. Instead, I revelled in the joy of playing with my vibrant, healthy children. It was a moment of bliss. But the instant I beheld my son on his deathbed, the fleeting joy I had experienced vanished like a wisp of smoke. At that moment, it felt as though I had lost not only my son but also all the beautiful children I had cherished in the sanctuary of my closed eyes."

With a heavy heart and a furrowed brow, Aditya's voice held a note of anguish as he grappled with the profound dilemma before him. "Which of these experiences is the truth? I find myself ensnared in a web of confusion, uncertain of how to reconcile these conflicting emotions. What path should I tread now, in the wake of this bewildering revelation?"

Aditya's words carried a profound weight of emotion as he pressed on, grappling with the agonising choices before him. "Should my tears fall for the child who now lies before me, or should they flow for the children I lost the moment I opened my eyes? In that sacred realm behind closed lids, I basked in happiness and revelled in a state of pure bliss. Yet, as soon as I dared to open my eyes, I was confronted with a world marred by suffering and agony. Two dreams, both vivid and yet worlds apart, unfolded within the realms of my consciousness. It dawns upon me that they are but dreams – one, a dream of unadulterated bliss, and the other, a haunting vision of suffering and pain."

Bhavya asked, "Guruji, how do sceptics challenge the validity of reincarnation claims, and how do proponents respond?"

Guruji's voice was steady, carrying the weight of centuries of inquiry.

"Bhavya, scepticism is not the enemy of truth—it is the fire that tests its strength, the chisel that sharpens understanding. Without doubt, there is no true search for knowledge; without questioning, there is no real faith. The greatest spiritual seekers in history were not those who blindly accepted, but those who dared to ask, to challenge, and to seek clarity beyond dogma."

He paused, his eyes reflecting the depth of his understanding.

"In the *Mahabharata* Bhagavad Gita 4:4, even Arjuna—the great warrior, the beloved disciple of Krishna—was filled with doubt on the battlefield of Kurukshetra. When Krishna spoke of the eternal soul, of reincarnation, of duty beyond life and death, Arjuna hesitated. He asked:

arjuna uvaacha

aparam bhavato janma param janma vivasvatah |

katham etad vijaaniyam tvam adau proktavaan iti | |

Meaning: 'How can I believe that you taught these truths to Vivasvan (the Sun God) in ancient times?

You were born in this age, while he was born long before you!'

Arjuna needed reassurance from Krishna. Krishna, rather than dismissing his doubt, answered him patiently, revealing the mystery of the soul's journey through countless lives. Doubt was not a weakness—it was the beginning of deeper understanding."

Guruji's gaze swept over the gathering, letting his words sink in.

"And look at Thomas, the disciple of Jesus. After the resurrection, when the others rejoiced at seeing Christ, Thomas refused to believe. He said:

'Unless I see the nail marks in his hands and put my finger where the nails were, and put my hand into his side, I will not believe.' (John 20:25)

Thomas was not condemned for his scepticism. Instead, when Jesus appeared to him, he offered his hands and his side, saying:

'Put your finger here; see my hands. Reach out your hand and put it into my side. Stop doubting and believe.' (John 20:27)

It was only through doubt that Thomas arrived at conviction, proclaiming: *'My Lord and my God!'*

Guruji's voice softened.

"Skepticism is not a rejection of truth—it is the yearning for a truth that is unshakable. Just as fire purifies gold, doubt refines our understanding. The Upanishads tell us:

'The wise do not blindly believe, nor do they dismiss. They inquire, they reflect, they experience.'

A true seeker does not reject an idea simply because it is beyond the realm of proof. Instead, they walk the path of experience, testing it in the fire of their own realisation."

He smiled gently.

"So, Bhavya, do not see doubt as an obstacle. See it as the lantern that lights the path. Let it lead you deeper until you find—not borrowed beliefs, not secondhand truths—but the wisdom that is your own."

The devotees listened, the air charged with quiet anticipation.

"Skeptics challenge reincarnation in many ways," Guruji continued. "They say, 'Where is the proof? Why do most people not remember past lives? If reincarnation is real, why do we not see it clearly in the present world?'

A scientist may argue that memories of past lives are nothing more than imagination—false recollections shaped by suggestion or cultural influence. A rationalist may call it wishful thinking, an attempt to escape the finality of death. A psychologist may explain it away as unconscious projections, childhood fantasies woven into vivid dreams."

He paused, then leaned forward slightly.

Guruji said. "There are hundreds of such accounts documented by researchers across the world—from the hills of Burma to the cities of Europe, from the villages of India to the streets of America. Dr. Ian Stevenson, a psychiatrist and researcher, spent decades studying these cases, meticulously verifying children's claims. The stories they told often aligned with real, deceased individuals. In some cases, children had birthmarks or physical traits corresponding to wounds or injuries from their alleged past lives."

Bhavya's brows furrowed. "But Guruji, how do the sceptics respond to these cases?"

Guruji nodded as if expecting the question.

"Skeptics argue that even hidden influences can explain these cases. They say children might overhear details from adults, unconsciously absorbing information that later emerges as 'memories.' Others claim these stories are culturally driven—that in societies where reincarnation is a common belief, children are more likely to fabricate such tales."

He let that thought linger for a moment.

"But I ask you," he said, his voice growing softer, "is everything that cannot be measured false? The wind cannot be seen, yet we feel its touch. Love cannot be dissected under a microscope, yet it moves mountains. The Taoists speak of *Qi*, the unseen force flowing through all things. And modern physics tells us that energy is never destroyed—it only changes form."

A gentle breeze rustled the trees as if the universe itself whispered in agreement.

"In the end, the debate between sceptics and believers is not about proof—it is about perception. The eyes will always seek tangible evidence, but the soul knows truths that cannot be written in numbers and equations.

So, I ask you, Bhavya—what is more reasonable? To believe that life is a flickering candle, extinguished forever at death? Or to believe that the flame is passed from one candle to another, continuing its journey through time?"

As the gentle drizzle caressed the earth, the devotees slowly dispersed from the Buddha Hall, their footsteps merging with the soft rhythm of the rain. The air was cool, carrying the scent of wet soil and blooming jasmine. Nita, wrapping her shawl tighter around her shoulders, turned to Akshaya and asked, "Why such a long break, Akshaya?"

Akshaya smiled knowingly. "Someone must be waiting for Guruji… perhaps someone in need of his presence."

A brief silence followed as if the rain itself acknowledged the weight of her words.

After a short reprieve, warmed by steaming chai and crisp evening snacks, a small group of devotees gathered under a modest shelter near Brindavan Garden. The twilight sky stretched in hues of deep indigo, the first stars timidly peeking through thinning clouds.

Vasudeva, who had been lost in thought, finally broke the silence. "Sam… what happened next?"

Sam exhaled slowly, his gaze distant, lost in a past he could neither change nor forget.

"I was adamant about starting my business, even though Amelia was not happy about it," he admitted. "She worried it would consume me. She feared success would demand sacrifices we weren't prepared for."

And she was right.

"The business grew rapidly. My days blurred into endless meetings, expansions, and strategies. I convinced myself I was building a future for both of us, yet, in reality, I was building a world where Amelia barely existed. She remained the same—gentle, patient, and endlessly giving—but I... I had become a visitor in my own home."

One evening, as we sat in our garden, Amelia broke the silence with a question that should have shaken me, but at the time, it did not.

"Sam, do you realise we don't have children?" she asked softly, staring at the horizon.

I laughed absentmindedly, sipping my tea. "Of course I do. But we have time, don't we? I know it gets lonely at home, but things will settle down soon. Everything will fall into place."

She smiled—one of those smiles that masked a thousand unspoken sorrows.

But things didn't fall into place.

They fell apart.

A few years passed, and Amelia began to grow weaker. It was subtle at first—her hands trembling slightly as she poured tea, her voice quieter, her steps slower. And then, one evening, without warning, she collapsed. The delicate porcelain cup shattered against the stone floor, and a thin stream of blood trickled from her nose.

Time froze.

In a blind panic, I rushed her to the hospital, my mind racing with questions, fears, and regrets I had no time to process. But nothing could have prepared me for what the doctor said next.

"Spend more time with your wife," the doctor advised, his tone gentle yet firm.

My breath caught in my throat. "What do you mean? Is she not alright?"

The doctor hesitated. "I thought you knew… Amelia has been battling cancer for two years."

The world tilted beneath my feet.

"She never told me," I whispered, my voice barely audible.

The doctor's expression softened. "Maybe she didn't want to burden you."

A sharp ache filled my chest, a weight pressing against my soul. How many moments had I missed? How many times had I been too busy to see what was right before me?

I pleaded, my voice cracking, "Doctor, please… do whatever it takes. I'll pay any price, move heaven and earth—just save her."

The doctor sighed. "The last hope is surgery, but the chances of survival are slim. A miracle."

A miracle.

All my life, I had believed success was the result of effort, of calculation, of perseverance. But now, standing at the precipice of loss, I realised life was not an equation to be solved—it was a fleeting gift, slipping through my fingers like sand.

I brought Amelia home, my hands trembling as I helped her onto the bed. The strong, composed man the world knew was gone. I wept—uncontrollably, shamelessly, desperately.

"I should have listened to you," I sobbed. "I wasted the time that was given to us."

Amelia, ever the pillar of grace, touched my face gently. Her eyes, though tired, held the same quiet strength.

"Who said I'm leaving you?" she whispered. "I will be with you until our old age."

I clung to those words, to that hope, refusing to surrender to fate.

I scoured the world for treatments, met with specialists, and researched every possible cure. I dedicated myself to one singular purpose: to keep her alive. Not for success, not for wealth, but for love—for the time I had once taken for granted.

The devotees sat in silence, absorbing the weight of my story. The sound of the rain had softened to a faint mist, the sky deepening into night.

Kiran sighed, glancing at his watch. "It's time… the session is about to begin."

Slowly, the group stood, but the air was thick with unspoken emotions. I remained still for a moment, my eyes fixed on the darkness beyond the garden, as if searching for something—perhaps for time lost or perhaps for Amelia's voice lingering in the wind.

And then, with a deep breath, I followed the others back toward the Buddha Hall, where Guruji's words awaited like a beacon in the night.

CHAPTER III
The Soul's Ultimate Destination

"The journey of the soul is not toward a final resting place, but toward the awakening of the infinite potential within, where liberation from the cycle of rebirth reveals the eternal truth of our existence."

– Shree Shambav

Synopsis

In this chapter, we explore the concept of the soul's ultimate goal, diving into the spiritual quest for union with the divine, eternal peace, or liberation from the cycle of rebirth. The chapter compares how different spiritual traditions—from Hinduism and Buddhism to Christianity and Islam—interpret enlightenment, salvation, and the soul's journey beyond earthly existence. Key concepts like **nirvana**, **moksha**, *and* **eternal peace** *are examined to understand their differing views on liberation and spiritual fulfilment. The chapter also considers the role of* **free will** *in shaping the soul's path toward its ultimate destination, emphasising the choices individuals make in their* *spiritual journey. Furthermore, personal experiences, mystical encounters, and spiritual insights are discussed as crucial factors that influence one's understanding of the soul's trajectory and ultimate destination. Through these varied perspectives, the chapter aims to offer a holistic view of the soul's journey, contemplating the possibilities of its final resting place or its merging with the divine.*

The air was thick with the scent of incense, and the rain outside had softened to a rhythmic whisper against the earth. The devotees sat in silence, their eyes fixed on Guruji.

Alice, her voice steady but filled with curiosity, asked, "Guruji, what is the soul's ultimate destination? Does it seek union with the divine, eternal peace, or freedom from this cycle of birth and death?"

Guruji closed his eyes for a moment, as if listening to something deeper than the words themselves. "Alice," he said gently, "imagine a river flowing through the valleys and plains, carving its way through mountains, meandering through forests, rushing in torrents, and at times resting in still pools. The river does not question its journey—it simply flows. And yet, no matter how vast the landscapes it travels, it is always moving toward the sea.

"The soul is that river. Some traditions call it Atman, others call it the essence, the divine spark, or the immortal self. Whatever name you give it, its journey is the same—seeking to return home. But what is home? That is where traditions differ, each offering a different vision of the ocean to which we return."

Guruji continued, "In Hindu thought, the goal of the soul is Moksha—liberation. Just as a dewdrop, after many cycles of evaporation and rainfall, ultimately merges with the vast ocean, so too does the soul seek to dissolve into Brahman, the infinite consciousness. It is not destruction, but the end of separation, the end of illusion. The self, once bound by karma, unshackles itself and awakens to its true nature."

He paused, allowing the thought to settle before moving on.

"In Buddhism, the journey is not towards union with God, but toward the extinguishing of suffering itself. Imagine a candle's flame, flickering in the wind—our cravings, attachments, and aversions keep it alight, keep us bound to this cycle of Samsara. Nirvana is when the flame is no longer needed, when there is nothing left to burn. It is not death, but freedom—the ultimate stillness where suffering ceases, where the self dissolves like mist in the morning sun."

Alice's brow furrowed slightly. "But Guruji, is Nirvana emptiness? Or is it a kind of eternal peace?"

Guruji smiled. "Imagine a wave rising from the ocean. For a moment, it has a form, an identity. It travels across the surface, dancing in the light, believing itself separate. But when it crashes upon the shore, does it disappear? No. It simply returns to the ocean. Was it ever truly apart? Or was it always the ocean in another form?

"In Nirvana, in Moksha, in enlightenment, the wave remembers its ocean nature. Whether you call it peace, liberation, or union, the essence is the same: the soul, after lifetimes of wandering, remembers what it truly is."

The hall was silent except for the sound of distant thunder, rolling low across the sky.

"But not all traditions see the journey this way," Guruji continued. "In Christianity, the soul longs for salvation—to stand in the presence of God, to be embraced by divine love, to enter the Kingdom of Heaven. The promise is not of dissolution, but of eternal communion. The soul does not disappear—it is recognised, known, and loved by its Creator. It is the prodigal son returning home after lifetimes of exile."

Alice's eyes glowed with understanding, but another question rose in her heart. "Guruji, what of those who do not seek Moksha, Nirvana, or Heaven? What of those who are still lost in the cycle?"

Guruji's voice softened, filled with both sorrow and compassion.

"A child lost in a vast marketplace may wander from stall to stall, enchanted by the colours, the music, the scent of food, and the promise of treasures. He forgets, for a time, that his home is elsewhere. But no matter how long he is lost, his mother never stops waiting for him."

"The soul may take lifetimes, even aeons, to remember its true nature. It may chase after desires, power, wealth, love, and knowledge—believing that fulfilment lies in these fleeting things. But just as a wave must return to the ocean, so too must the soul, in time, seek its return.

"Some wake up in one lifetime. Others take many. But eternity is patient."

The hall remained still, the moment stretched like a fragile thread between past and present. Alice bowed her head, absorbing the depth of Guruji's words.

"Guruji," she whispered, "how does one begin the journey back?"

Guruji's smile was gentle, like the first light of dawn.

"You already have, Alice. The moment you ask the question, the path has begun."

Guruji said, "Let me narrate a story."

The Lost River

There was once a river, born high in the mountains, where the air was thin and the sky kissed the earth. She began as a mere trickle, a fragile whisper of water that danced over stones, laughing in the sunlight. As she flowed downward, she grew, her currents strengthening, carving her way through valleys, meadows, and forests.

The river loved her journey. She adored the way she could shape the land, nourish the trees, and cradle the fish within her depths. She became vast and mighty, her waters carrying stories of the world itself. But as she travelled, she began to forget where she had come from.

One day, as she reached the plains, she saw a great desert ahead. It stretched endlessly before her, dry and vast. For the first time, fear entered her heart.

"What will happen if I cross the desert?" she wondered. "Will I disappear? Will I cease to be?"

She hesitated at the edge, uncertain. And so, she did what many before she had done—she searched for meaning.

The Many Paths

The river came across a sage meditating by her banks.

"O wise one," she asked, "what is my destiny?"

The sage smiled. "You seek the ocean," he said, "but you fear losing yourself. Do not be afraid. The ocean is not the end—it is the beginning. You are not separate from it. You are the ocean in another form."

The river was puzzled. "But I have spent my whole existence as a river. If I surrender, will I still be me?"

The sage only chuckled and returned to his meditation.

Determined to find her own answers, the river continued onward.

She met a village by her banks, where people spoke of a great kingdom beyond the desert.

"There is a land where the Creator waits for us," an old woman told her. "He does not wish for you to disappear—He wants you to be known, to be loved. If you are faithful, you will be welcomed into His eternal embrace."

The river hesitated. "But what of the ocean?"

The old woman shook her head. "The ocean is empty. The kingdom is full."

Conflicted, the river moved on.

Further down, she met a traveller who told her a different tale.

"Life is suffering," he said, gazing at the horizon. "We flow, we crash, we evaporate, we return—all because we are bound by longing, by attachment. If you wish to be free, you must cease to flow altogether. Let the thirst of the desert swallow you. Let the sun take you. Then, you will no longer be bound."

The river trembled. "But what will I become?"

The traveller only smiled.

The river continued her journey, carrying these stories in her depths, yet uncertain of her own truth.

The Surrender

At last, she reached the desert. The heat bore down upon her, and she felt herself beginning to fade. The more she tried to hold herself together, the more she fragmented.

And then, she heard a voice—a whisper on the wind.

"Do not resist."

The river stilled.

"Let go," the voice murmured, "and you will see."

Taking a trembling breath, the river surrendered.

She let herself rise, lifted by the warm embrace of the sun. She felt herself transform, no longer a current, no longer a river—but something greater. She became the very breath of the sky, carried by the wind, travelling vast distances, weightless and free.

And then, as if by some ancient memory, she felt herself drawn back to the mountains. She fell once more as rain, kissing the earth, becoming a stream, flowing once again towards the sea.

And at last, she understood.

She had never been lost. She had never truly disappeared. She had always been the ocean—whether as a river, as mist, or as rain.

The ocean was not the end.

It was home.

The Return to the Present

Guruji's voice faded into the silence of the hall. The devotees sat still, their hearts carrying the weight of the story.

Alice wiped away a tear she hadn't realised had fallen.

"So," she whispered, "no matter what path we take—whether we seek Nirvana, Moksha, Heaven, or peace—we all return?"

Guruji nodded. "Yes, Alice. Some take lifetimes. Some take moments. Some dissolve like the wave, others stand in the light of the Divine. But in the end, the journey is the same.

"We do not disappear.

"We return."

A hush fell upon the room, deep as the ocean itself.

The air in the ashram was thick with the scent of sandalwood and the quiet hum of life settling into the evening's rhythm. Sofia, her voice steady yet filled with the quiet tremor of deep curiosity, asked, *"Guruji, what do various spiritual traditions define as the soul's ultimate goal—such as enlightenment, salvation, or union with the divine?"*

Guruji remained silent for a moment, his eyes gazing far beyond the horizon. Then, with a slow, measured breath, he spoke.

"Imagine, Sofia, that you are a drop of water suspended in the air, having fallen from the vast ocean.

You travel through the skies and become part of a river, a stream, or a raindrop, but no matter where you go, there is always an unshakable longing—a whisper in the depths of your being that calls you home. This longing is the soul's journey."

The devotees leaned in, drawn into the depth of his words.

"Different traditions name this return differently, yet all speak of the same essence. The Buddhists call it Nirvana—the extinguishing of the self's illusions, like a candle merging into the vast light of truth. It is not an ending, but a liberation from suffering, from the cycle of birth and death. To realise Nirvana is to wake up from the dream of separation, to see clearly that there was never any distance between the drop and the ocean."

He paused, allowing the words to settle like ripples on still water.

"In Hinduism, we speak of Moksha—the breaking of the karmic cycle, the soul's liberation from the bindings of this world. It is like a bird, caged for lifetimes, finally remembering the vast sky it belongs to. Moksha is the recognition that the Atman, the individual soul, is not separate from Brahman, the Supreme Consciousness. The journey was never about reaching something new, but about peeling away the layers of illusion that made you forget who you truly are."

A gentle breeze stirred the temple bells, their chime blending with the distant calls of night birds.

"In Christianity," he continued, "the soul seeks salvation—a return to the divine presence of God. It is a journey of grace, of surrender, of love that redeems. Just as a lost child is embraced by the arms of a loving parent, so too does the soul, through faith and devotion, find its way back to the eternal home."

His eyes softened, gazing at the flames dancing in the oil lamps.

"In Sufism, this longing is a divine romance—the soul is the lover, aching for reunion with the Beloved. The great mystics spoke of annihilation in divine love, of dissolving so completely that only God remains. The way a moth is drawn to the flame, the soul is irresistibly pulled toward the source of all existence."

The silence that followed was deep and reverent. Even the wind seemed to be still, listening.

Then, Guruji smiled—a quiet, knowing smile.

"But tell me, Sofia," he said gently, *"do you truly believe the drop was ever separate from the ocean?"*

Sofia's breath caught in her throat. The question was simple, yet it unravelled something vast within her.

"What if," Guruji continued, *"the soul's journey is not about travelling a great distance, but about remembering? What if enlightenment, salvation, union—whatever name we give it—is simply the recognition that you have never been apart from the divine? That you, in this very moment, are already there?"*

The fire crackled softly. Somewhere in the distance, the call of a nightingale rose into the darkening sky.

No one spoke. No one moved.

And in that silence, something shifted—not in the world outside, but in the universe within.

Sam leaned forward, his brow furrowed with the weight of a question that had been circling his mind. He took a slow breath, then finally spoke. *"Guruji, how do concepts like nirvana, moksha, and eternal peace differ in their explanations of liberation?"*

Guruji, who had been gazing into the flame of an oil lamp before him, slowly lifted his eyes to meet Sam's. There was something ancient in his gaze—something vast and unbound by time. He let the silence linger for a moment before answering.

"Sam, imagine three travellers lost in a great desert. The sun scorches their backs, and their throats burn with thirst. They search desperately for water, for relief, for a way out of this endless expanse of suffering."

The devotees listened, their breaths caught in the net of his words.

"The first traveller stumbles upon an oasis. As he drinks, he feels the coolness rush through him, extinguishing his suffering. He realises the thirst was only an illusion, that the water had always been there, waiting for him to see it. This is Nirvana."

He paused, his voice as calm as the wind that carried the scent of jasmine through the open courtyard.

"Nirvana, as the Buddhists understand it, is the cessation of suffering. It is not a place one reaches, but a state of awakening—like a flame that, once extinguished, no longer flickers in the winds of desire, attachment, and illusion. It is the realisation that suffering only exists because we cling to that which is impermanent. When clinging stops, suffering ceases. The traveller does not escape the desert; he sees through the illusion that he was lost at all."

Sam exhaled softly, absorbing the depth of the analogy.

Guruji continued, his voice gentle yet resonant.

"The second traveller walks for what seems like lifetimes. He searches tirelessly, his feet blistered from the journey. Then, finally, he reaches the edge of the desert. Before him lies an endless, shimmering ocean. He takes one step forward, then another, until he dissolves into the waves, becoming one with the infinite. This is Moksha."

A hush fell over the gathering, as if the very air bowed in reverence to the wisdom being unveiled.

"In Hinduism," Guruji explained, *"Moksha is liberation from the cycle of birth and death, from karma, from illusion. It is the ultimate homecoming—the realisation that the Atman, the individual soul, was never separate from Brahman, the Supreme Consciousness. The drop of water does not fear dissolving into the ocean, for it was always the ocean."*

"And the third traveller?" Sam asked, his voice barely above a whisper.

Guruji's lips curved into the faintest smile.

"The third traveller," he said, *"does not seek an oasis. He does not walk toward the ocean. He sits beneath the shade of a lone tree, closes his eyes, and breathes. He embraces the desert as it is. He no longer sees suffering, nor liberation—only peace. This is eternal peace, the state that some spiritual traditions, like certain schools of Daoism and Christianity, describe as the ultimate rest in God, in the flow of existence itself."*

Sam, his heart full, looked up at Guruji, his voice hushed yet resolute.

"So the goal is different for each traveller?"

Guruji's eyes softened a quiet understanding within them.

"Or perhaps, Sam, the goal is the same. It is only the path that differs."

Akshaya asked Guruji, his voice steady yet filled with quiet wonder. "Guruji, what role does free will play in determining the soul's path toward its ultimate destination?"

Guruji remained still, his eyes half-closed, as if he had already seen the question long before it had been spoken. Then, with a serene smile, he looked up.

"Akshaya, imagine a mighty river," he began, his voice a gentle current guiding them toward deeper waters. "It begins as a mere trickle in the mountains, fed by melting snow, by rain, by unseen springs deep beneath the earth. From its very birth, it is destined for the ocean—it cannot escape this truth. But tell me, does the river not carve its own course?"

Akshaya's breath caught slightly. The devotees leaned in, drawn by the gravity of the moment.

"The river may take the most direct path, flowing smoothly toward the vast embrace of the sea. Or it may twist and turn, carving valleys, shaping landscapes, surrendering to obstacles, yet never ceasing its journey. Some rivers dry up for a time, lost beneath the desert sands, only to rise again in another place, in another form. Some grow wild, unpredictable, flooding their banks, while others move with slow grace, nourishing all they touch."

He paused, letting his words sink in like rain upon thirsty earth.

"But no matter the path it chooses, the river will always meet the ocean. The soul, too, is bound for its ultimate destination—be it union with the Divine, moksha, enlightenment, or an eternal return home. This is destiny. Yet, within this destiny, the soul has free will—just as the river chooses its course, the soul chooses how it will travel."

Akshaya's eyes shimmered with something unspeakable—an understanding that was both thrilling and humbling.

"So, Guruji," he asked, his voice barely above a whisper, *"is free will an illusion, then? If the river is destined for the ocean, do its choices truly matter?"*

A slow smile spread across Guruji's face, as if he had been waiting for this very question.

"Ah, Akshaya," he said softly, "tell me—does the way you walk a journey matter less than the destination itself? If you must travel to the peak of a sacred mountain, does it not make a difference whether you choose the steepest, most arduous path or the one lined with flowers and shaded trees? Does it not shape your experience? The journey sculpts the traveller, just as the river shapes the land it flows through."

He leaned forward slightly, his gaze steady.

"Free will does not change the ocean. But it changes you."

A deep silence settled among the devotees. The fire crackled again, sending a brief cascade of sparks into the sky, as if the universe itself were answering.

"Some souls choose love, others choose fear. Some choose wisdom, others choose ignorance. But all choices, whether light or shadow, whether detour or direct path, ultimately lead to the same truth. The ocean does not reject the river, no matter how long it wanders."

Akshaya felt her heart swell, her mind unravelling its tightly held fears.

"So, Guruji… in the end, we are always free, yet always guided?"

Guruji nodded, his face glowing with an inner light.

"Yes. Like a bird is free to ride the wind in any direction, yet cannot fly beyond the sky itself. Like a traveller who can take any road, yet all roads will one day bring them home."

The night was wrapped in a soft hush, the kind of silence that wasn't empty but pregnant with meaning, like the pause between the notes of a sacred melody. The wind carried the scent of night-blooming jasmine, and somewhere in the distance, the rhythmic chant of a lone seeker whispered through the darkness.

Vasudeva, his voice was steady but carried the weight of an unspoken yearning. "Guruji, how do personal experiences, mystical encounters, or spiritual insights influence one's understanding of the soul's journey and destination?"

"Ah, Vasudeva," Guruji said gently, "if I were to describe the ocean to a man who had never seen it, could mere words ever be enough?"

Vasudeva hesitated before shaking his head.

"You see," Guruji continued, *"one may read a thousand scriptures, listen to countless discourses, and engage in endless debates about the nature of the soul's journey. But a single moment of true experience—a glimpse beyond the veil—can transform understanding in ways words never could."*

He paused, his eyes scanning the small gathering before him.

"Let me tell you a story," he said, his voice slipping into the cadence of memory.

There was once a young seeker named Arjuna, who travelled far and wide, searching for the truth. He visited temples, sat with sages, and memorised sacred texts. He could recite every verse on moksha, nirvana, and the eternal soul. Yet, his heart remained restless. The knowledge filled his mind, but his soul still thirsted.

One day, weary from his quest, he found himself in the heart of a dense forest. There, he encountered an old hermit who sat in perfect stillness, his eyes reflecting the depth of a thousand lifetimes. Arjuna, eager to prove his wisdom, began speaking of the soul's journey, quoting the scriptures flawlessly.

The hermit listened patiently. When Arjuna finished, the old man smiled and said, "You speak beautifully, my child. But tell me, what does water taste like?"

Arjuna frowned. "Water?" he repeated. "Water has no taste."

The hermit nodded. "Yet, if you are parched in the desert, does a sip of water not feel sweeter than honey?"

Arjuna hesitated.

"You have read about water, described it, debated it, but you have never truly been thirsty enough to know it."

Then, without warning, the hermit reached out and pushed Arjuna into the nearby river.

Arjuna flailed, gasping for air, his body overcome with panic. He struggled, his chest tightening as the water swallowed him. And just as he felt he would drown, the hermit pulled him back to the shore.

Coughing and trembling, Arjuna looked at the hermit, anger rising in his chest.

"Why did you do that?" he demanded.

The hermit only smiled.

"Did you think about scripture when you were drowning?" he asked softly. "Did you recite verses on the nature of the soul, or did you only crave one thing?"

Arjuna, still catching his breath, whispered, "Air."

"And now," the hermit said, "you understand devotion. You understand longing. When your thirst for truth becomes as desperate as your need for air, when the soul aches for the divine as a drowning man aches for breath, then—only then—you will know."

Guruji's voice softened as he returned to the present.

"Vasudeva, the soul's journey is not an abstract idea. It is lived. It is felt. It is experienced. A man can speak of love, but only the one who has loved knows its fire. A seeker can discuss liberation, but only the one who has touched that infinite silence knows its depth."

The devotees sat in stunned silence, each of them turning inward, lost in the meaning of his words.

"Mystical experiences, profound realisations, moments when time ceases and the universe reveals itself in a whisper—these shape our path more than any teaching ever could. They are the soul's way of remembering where it has come from and where it must return."

Vasudeva's eyes glistened with unshed tears. He had spent so long searching for truth in words, in logic, in reason. But tonight, under the vastness of the sky, with Guruji's words sinking into his being, he felt something shift—like a door unlocking within his soul.

After a long pause, Guruji slowly rose from his asana, signalling the end of the day's session. His movements were unhurried, his presence still resonating in the silence that followed. As the devotees bowed in reverence, the session dissolved into quiet reflection.

The Night Whispers of Fate

Later that evening, after a fulfilling meal, Akshaya and the others gathered around the fireplace. The fire crackled softly, casting golden embers into the night air, each spark rising like a fleeting prayer before vanishing into the vast darkness. The sky stretched above them, a silent witness adorned with a thousand shimmering stars. Fireflies floated like tiny lanterns, flickering in rhythm with the nocturnal symphony—the distant croaking of frogs, the rustling of leaves in the cool breeze, the faint trickle of water weaving its melody through the night.

Nature was awake, humming its eternal song.

Akshaya, Sujitha, Espen, and Astyn sat deep in discussion, their voices laced with the echoes of Guruji's teachings from earlier that day. Nearby, Padma, Apeksha, and Akshatha joined them, their eyes reflecting the gentle glow of the fire.

Apeksha turned to Sam, curiosity in her voice. **"Sam, what happened next?"**

Sam took a deep breath, gazing into the flames as if searching for the past within them. The firelight danced across his face, revealing emotions too deep for words.

A Chance Meeting, A Fated Path

"It was accidental," Sam began. "Or maybe it wasn't."

"I first heard about Guruji from an old friend—someone I had lost touch with for years. Life had taken us in different directions, and I had not spoken to him in what felt like another lifetime. But one day, out of nowhere, he reached out. He told me about Guruji, about his wisdom, his presence, and how his words had transformed lives."

Sam exhaled slowly, his voice carrying the weight of memories.

"There was something in his voice—a conviction, a certainty—that made me pause. And in that moment, something stirred within me, a knowing beyond logic, beyond reason. I turned to Amelia and said, 'Let's go. Let's meet him.'"

We had travelled to Kanchipuram, a place that breathed peace. The very air seemed to hum with a quiet, healing energy.

"Amelia stood at the entrance of the ashram, her eyes wide with wonder. 'I have never seen such serenity in my life,' she whispered."

For the first time in a long while, Sam had felt something shift—an anticipation, a silent promise of something greater than himself.

The Meeting That Changed Everything

"When we finally stood before Guruji, he looked at Amelia with a gaze so deep, so knowing, that it felt as if he saw beyond flesh and bone—straight into her soul."

Guruji had spoken in his calm, unwavering voice:

"What you believe will happen. You are the creator of your reality. You shape your world with your thoughts. Your manifestation will work."

He closed his eyes for a brief moment, the air around them growing still, as if the very universe were listening. Then he opened them and said with certainty,

"Go ahead with the surgery. We will meet after. You will be whole again, Amelia. You will be healed."

Tears welled up in Sam's eyes as he looked at Guruji. His voice cracked as he whispered, *"I want Amelia... I cannot lose her."*

Guruji's smile was gentle, yet it carried an ocean of wisdom. "We neglect what is closest to us, Sam. And when we feel we are about to lose it, we fight desperately to hold on. Life teaches us through absence what we fail to cherish in presence. But have faith. Amelia has a strong will. She will overcome this."

Then, with infinite tenderness, Guruji placed his hand on Amelia's head.

Amelia shivered. Tears streamed down her face, but for the first time in years, they were not tears of pain or fear. They were tears of release, of surrender. She felt something lift, something unburdening itself from her very being.

"Guruji… you have given me back my lost happiness," she whispered.

Guruji simply smiled and left, his presence lingering like a quiet blessing.

A Second Chance at Life

"The surgery happened," Sam said, his voice thick with emotion. "And against all odds, she survived. Not only did she survive, but she healed in ways I never imagined. And you all saw her at our last retreat. She was glowing—alive in a way she hadn't been in years."

A deep silence settled over the group. The wind carried Sam's words, weaving them into the fabric of the night, carrying them beyond the trees, beyond the hills, to places unseen.

Sam exhaled, his gaze lifting to the endless expanse of stars above them. "I learned one thing," he said. "Life should never be taken for granted. Because if we do, it will teach us the hard way. It will take, and when we finally wake up, we will realise that we spent too much time looking away."

He looked at each of them, his voice steady now.

"We all chase something—money, success, power, distractions. And we tell ourselves, 'Later. There will be time later.' But what if there isn't? What if the people we love, the life we are meant to cherish, slip through our fingers while we are too busy looking elsewhere?"

His voice softened.

"Amelia always asks me, 'What would have happened if we had never met Guruji?' And every time, I have no answer. Because that meeting didn't just save her life. It saved mine."

The devotees sat in utter silence, their hearts heavy with unspoken thoughts, their eyes reflecting the starlit sky above. It was as if even the universe had paused, listening to the story that had just unfolded.

The fire crackled once more, its embers rising, vanishing into the night.

The wind sighed as if carrying prayers to distant lands.

And slowly, one by one, the devotees rose, retreating into the embrace of the night, their hearts fuller, their breaths deeper, their souls touched by the weight of a truth they could never unlearn.

SECTION TWO

Embracing Death as a Teacher

"Death is not a foe to fear, but a wise teacher who guides us to understand the impermanence of life, the preciousness of each moment, and the eternal truths that lie beyond the physical realm."

-Shree Shambav

CHAPTER IV
Life Lessons from Death

"In facing death, we come to understand that what we leave behind is not material wealth, but the love we've shared, the wisdom we've imparted, and the marks we've made on the souls of those we've touched."

– Shree Shambav

Synopsis

*This chapter explores how understanding the nature of death and the afterlife can profoundly transform the way we live. It delves into the role of death awareness in inspiring a more purposeful and authentic life. By contemplating the inevitability of death, individuals can awaken to the preciousness of time and the importance of living with intention. The chapter examines how an understanding of **impermanence** can reduce fear and attachment, allowing for a greater sense of peace and acceptance in the face of life's uncertainties. Additionally, it explores how the concepts of **karma** and **soul growth** shape our decisions, actions, and relationships, helping us to live more ethically and compassionately. Finally, the chapter reflects on how contemplating death and the afterlife can deepen our appreciation* *for the present moment, urging us to fully engage with life as it unfolds. In sum, this chapter illustrates that through the lens of death, we can learn to live with greater clarity, connection, and purpose.*

Astyn awoke with a quiet thrill stirring in her heart, a sense of anticipation humming through her being. It was as if something unseen yet deeply known was calling her, whispering to the deepest chambers of her soul. As she stepped out of her room, the ashram was already alive, moving in harmony with the quiet rhythm of the morning.

The darkness of night was dissolving, retreating into the folds of the universe, as the first golden fingers of dawn stretched across the sky. A soft mist hovered over the earth, kissing the dewy grass, as birds hidden in the canopies began their morning symphony. Their songs wove effortlessly with the low, resonant chants of *OM* reverberating from the meditation hall, the sacred sound rolling like a wave across the ashram, filling every space with an inexplicable serenity. The lingering aroma of sandalwood incense curled through the air, merging with the fresh scent of wet earth, the fragrance wrapping around her like an unspoken blessing.

Astyn inhaled deeply, her chest rising and falling with a breath that felt older than time itself. At that moment, something shifted within her—a profound stillness, a quiet ecstasy that had no name.

Lalitha stood beside her, equally entranced by the sacred beauty unfolding before them. She exhaled, her voice barely above a whisper, as though afraid to disturb the delicate harmony of the moment.

"This place is tranquil… There is so much to learn from nature, from this deep silence."

A sudden breeze stirred the leaves, brushing against Astyn's skin like an unseen hand, whispering truths that could not be spoken but only felt. Her eyes welled up, not from sorrow, but from something vast and ungraspable—an overwhelming awe, a recognition of something eternal. She let the tears flow, unbidden, as goosebumps prickled her arms. For the first time in her life, the world felt utterly complete, as though she were standing at the threshold of a great revelation.

As if drawn by an unseen force, others began to gather. Akshaya and Vasudeva arrived, their faces alight with quiet contemplation. Padma, Abhirami, and Sofia joined them, their expressions reflecting the same unspoken understanding—a deep knowing beyond words.

Soon, the morning led them towards the meditation hall, their footsteps merging with the rhythmic stillness of the ashram. As they entered, they saw Akshatha and Apeksha already seated in meditation, their forms motionless as statues, radiating an aura of peace. Around them, devotees engaged in their morning *sadhana*—some flowing through sacred yoga postures with devotion, others lost in the art of breathwork, their inhalations and exhalations merging seamlessly with the rhythm of the universe.

From one corner of the ashram, the deep hum of *OM* resonated, its vibration expanding outward like ripples in a still pond. From another, the soulful notes of a bhajan floated through the air, accompanied by the gentle strumming of a *tanpura* and the resonant beats of a *mridangam*. The entire space was alive with divinity—a celestial orchestra where silence and sound danced together in perfect harmony.

Wandering further, they reached the Brindavan Garden, where the day was unfurling in all its splendour. The sun's early rays filtered through the dense foliage, casting intricate golden patterns on the earth. Flowers swayed in the gentle breeze, their petals adorned with the last remnants of dawn's dewdrops. The intoxicating scent of jasmine, roses, and tulsi filled the air, carrying with it whispers of ancient wisdom. Nearby, Astha and others tended to the garden with reverence, their hands moving over the soil with a tenderness that felt like prayer. Each act was sacred, each moment an offering.

The morning had unfolded like a sacred hymn—each breath, each movement a verse in an eternal song. The world was not merely alive; it was divine.

With hearts full and minds stilled, they returned to their rooms to prepare for the revered morning session. Their steps felt lighter, as though they were walking not merely toward the hall but toward something infinitely greater—something beyond knowledge, beyond words, beyond the self.

When they finally entered the Buddha Hall, a hush settled over the gathering. Guruji sat before them, draped in simplicity, his presence alone commanding silence. He remained still for a long moment, as though listening to something beyond the physical realm. Then, folding his hands, he began the morning prayer, his voice carrying the weight of ancient wisdom.

A subtle shift in the air, a collective inhalation. The devotees closed their eyes, not merely as an act of devotion, but as a surrender to something vast and eternal.

The room grew heavy with an almost tangible energy—an anticipation so deep it felt as though the very air was listening. Time itself seemed to bow in reverence.

Akanksh, his voice steady but reflective, broke the silence.

"Guruji," he asked, "how can an awareness of death's inevitability inspire us to live more purposefully and authentically?"

Guruji gazed at him for a moment, his expression neither sorrowful nor joyful, but vast—like the sky before a storm, holding something profound.

The Story of the Candle and the Wind

"There was once a young prince," Guruji began, "who lived in a kingdom of endless pleasures. His days were filled with music and feasts, his nights with the glow of golden lanterns and the laughter of friends. He never gave death a second thought, for why would he? He was young, and life stretched before him like an endless road."

"But one day, a sage visited the palace. He was old—so old that his skin was like parchment, his hair silver as moonlight. The prince, amused, asked him, 'Old man, what wisdom do you carry in that frail body of yours?'"

"The sage smiled and held up a single candle. 'Tell me, Prince,' he said, 'if this flame knew the wind was coming to extinguish it, would it burn differently?'"

"The prince frowned. 'What does it matter? A flame is a flame, whether it burns a second or a lifetime.'"

"The sage nodded. 'Ah, but would it dance more fiercely? Would it give more light while it still could? Or would it flicker in fear, shrinking from the wind?'"

"The prince had no answer. He had never thought of life that way."

The Awakening

"One evening, as the prince rode through his kingdom, he saw a funeral procession. A man wrapped in white cloth was being carried to the river, his loved ones walking beside him, heads bowed. The prince watched in silence. He had seen many celebrations, but this was different. There were no songs, no feasts—only the quiet sound of feet on dust and the weeping of those left behind."

"That night, he could not sleep. The image of the burning candle haunted him. The wind would come for him, too. Maybe not today, maybe not tomorrow—but it would come."

"The thought terrified him. Had he truly lived? Had he loved deeply enough, laughed loudly enough? Had he seen the world beyond the palace walls, beyond his own comforts?"

"And so, the next morning, he made a choice."

"He left behind his silks and jewels. He walked barefoot through the villages and listened to the stories of the poor, the sick, the forgotten. He sat with the dying, holding their hands as their breaths slowed. And in their eyes, he saw something he had never seen before."

"Not fear."

"But peace."

"They had lived. They had held their children, sung their songs, toiled under the sun, and wept under the stars. They had known love, pain, longing, and fulfilment. They did not regret the wind's arrival. They had burned brightly, and that was enough."

The Truth of the Flame

Guruji paused, letting the silence settle over the room like a warm embrace.

"The awareness of death," he finally said, "is not meant to paralyse us—it is meant to awaken us. It is not a shadow looming over us, but a whisper reminding us to live."

"When we know the candle will not burn forever, we cherish its light. We let it illuminate the faces of those we love. We do not waste time in anger, in meaningless pursuits, in delaying happiness for 'someday.' Because someday is uncertain. But now—this moment—is real."

He looked at Akanksh, his eyes filled with something deep and unwavering.

"So, my child, do not fear the wind. Let your flame dance. Let it burn with passion, with kindness, with truth. That way, when the wind finally comes, you will not tremble.

You will shine."

The hall remained silent, but the air was alive with something unspoken.

Akanksh exhaled, as if he had been holding a weight within him. He bowed his head slightly, and Guruji smiled.

Outside, the wind whispered through the trees, carrying the scent of jasmine and the echoes of a flame that refused to be afraid.

Lalitha, her voice thoughtful yet yearning, asked, "Guruji, what role does understanding impermanence play in reducing fear and attachment in daily life?"

Guruji closed his eyes for a moment, then began, his voice calm and measured.

The Story of the River and the Sky

"There was once a river that loved the land it flowed through. It cradled the roots of great trees, carried the whispers of fish, and glistened under the warmth of the sun. It felt at home between its banks, winding through valleys and villages, feeding all that lived along its shores."

"But one day, the river noticed something that troubled it deeply. The banks that held it were slowly eroding, and the trees it had once nourished were shedding their leaves and standing bare. The river wept, for it did not want to lose what it loved. It clung desperately to its shape, trying to slow its own current, fearing the day it might disappear."

"The sky, watching from above, saw the river's sorrow. One evening, as the sun dipped below the horizon, the sky spoke."

"'Why do you fear change, dear river?' the sky asked."

"'Because everything I love is slipping away,' the river replied. 'I do not want to lose the trees, the banks, the creatures that call me home.'"

"The sky, full of stars now, smiled. 'But dear river, do you not see? You are not losing anything. You are becoming something greater. One day, the sun will draw you into its warmth, lifting you beyond these banks, carrying you to distant lands where you will fall as rain, feeding forests you have never seen, filling lakes that will give life to others. You will not end—you will transform.'"

"The river fell silent. It had spent so long fearing the loss of what it was, that it had never considered what it could become."

The Truth of Impermanence

Guruji opened his eyes, gazing at Lalitha with a look of deep understanding.

"Lalitha, we are all rivers. We flow through this life, touching those we love, shaping the world around us, believing that if we could just hold on tightly enough, we could stop time itself. But time is not something to be stopped. It is the current that carries us home."

"When we cling—whether to people, possessions, identities, or even our own youth—we suffer. We suffer because we resist what is natural: the unfolding of life. We fear impermanence, yet it is impermanence that allows everything to exist at all."

He gestured toward the lamp's flame, its light dancing.

"This flame will not burn forever. And yet, while it does, it gives warmth, it illuminates the room, it touches our lives. Should we grieve because it will one day flicker out, or should we cherish its glow while it still burns?"

Lalitha's eyes glistened as she absorbed his words.

"So, Guruji… if we truly accept impermanence, we won't fear losing things?"

Guruji chuckled softly.

"No, my child. You will still love. You will still grieve. But your love will be purer, and your grief will be gentler. You will no longer hold on out of fear, but out of gratitude. You will love without possession. You will live without clinging. And when the time comes to let go, you will do so with grace, knowing that nothing is ever truly lost—only transformed."

Silence settled in the hall, but it was not empty. It was full—full of something unspoken yet deeply felt.

Lalitha bowed her head, and Guruji smiled once more.

Sujitha, her eyes filled with curiosity, leaned forward and asked, "Guruji, how can reflecting on karma and soul growth influence our decisions and relationships?"

Guruji nodded as if she had touched upon something profound.

"There was once a master weaver named Zilpah, who lived in a quiet village. She was known for creating the most intricate and beautiful tapestries, each thread woven with such care that her work seemed to breathe with life."

"One day, a young girl named Meera approached her and said, 'Master, teach me to weave as you do.'"

"Zilpah smiled and handed her a single thread. 'Before you can weave a tapestry, you must understand the thread. Hold it. Look at it.'"

"Meera frowned. 'It is just a thread. It is too small to matter.'"

"Zilpah chuckled and said, 'Come back tomorrow, and I will show you something.'"

"The next day, when Meera returned, Zilpah showed her two tapestries. One was flawless, its patterns flowing harmoniously like a river's song. The other was tangled, knotted, and broken in places."

"'What do you see?' Zilpah asked."

"Meera pointed to the broken one. 'This one is ruined.'"

"Zilpah nodded. 'Yes. And do you know why? Because one thread was not placed with care. When a single thread is knotted or frayed, it affects the whole design. That is how karma works, my child. Every action, every word, every thought—it is a thread in the tapestry of your life. If woven with mindfulness, it creates something beautiful. If woven carelessly, it tangles, leaving you to unravel the knots later.'"

Karma and the Weaving of Our Lives

Guruji paused, letting the story settle into the minds of those listening. Then, he spoke again, his voice gentle.

"Sujitha, every choice we make, every word we speak, every emotion we nurture—it all weaves the fabric of our existence. Karma is not some cosmic punishment, nor is it merely a reward. It is simply cause and effect, action and consequence. The soul does not grow through punishment; it grows through understanding."

"When we reflect on karma, we begin to see our relationships differently. We stop reacting blindly. We ask, 'What kind of thread am I weaving here?' If we weave with anger, we create knots of pain. If we weave with kindness, we create patterns of harmony."

He gestured toward the lamp's flickering flame.

"Imagine a person who is impatient and harsh with others. He speaks without thought, wounds without care. Each word is a knot in the tapestry. One day, he finds himself surrounded by broken relationships, by resentment and loneliness. He wonders, 'Why has life been so cruel to me?' But life was not cruel. He simply wove his own sorrow without realising it."

"But then, imagine someone who, even in moments of frustration, pauses. She chooses patience. She chooses compassion. She chooses to see beyond her own ego. She weaves her tapestry with golden threads of understanding. Years later, she finds herself surrounded by warmth, by love, by peace. Not by accident—but because of the choices she made."

The Reflection of the Soul

Sujitha's eyes were moist now, as if something within her had been awakened.

"So, Guruji… karma is not about fate? It is about the patterns we create?"

Guruji smiled.

"Yes, my child. Karma is not written in stone. It is written in thread. And with awareness, we can always choose to weave a new pattern. The soul does not grow by wishing for better circumstances—it grows by weaving better actions, moment by moment, lifetime by lifetime."

Silence followed, but it was the kind of silence that hummed with realisation.

Espen, a seeker with eyes full of questions, leaned forward and asked, "Guruji, in what ways can the study of death and the afterlife deepen our appreciation for the present moment?"

Guruji's gaze settled on him, deep and knowing. He took a long breath, as if inhaling the weight of lifetimes, then smiled—a slow, sorrowful, and yet infinitely tender smile.

The Story of the Last Cup of Tea

"There was once a master named Haruto," Guruji began. "He was known far and wide, not just for his wisdom but for the peace that radiated from him, like a lantern in the dark."

"One day, a troubled young man came to him and said, 'Master, I cannot find peace. My mind is always restless, either drowning in the past or fearing the future. How do I learn to live in the present?'"

"Haruto, without a word, poured him a cup of tea."

"The young man watched as the tea flowed, its steam curling like ghostly fingers in the air. Just as the cup was about to overflow, Haruto stopped and placed it before him."

"'Drink this tea,' Haruto said. 'But drink it as if it were your last cup.'"

"The young man frowned, confused. 'But… it is just tea.'"

"Haruto chuckled. 'Yes. But if you knew this was the last tea you would ever taste—the last warmth upon your lips, the last fragrance in your nostrils, the last moment your hands would cradle a cup—would it still be *just tea*?'"

"The young man hesitated. He lifted the cup with reverence, feeling the delicate ceramic, noticing the way the light reflected off its rim. He took a slow sip, truly tasting the tea for the first time in his life. The warmth spread through him, and suddenly, tears welled in his eyes."

"'Master… this tea is exquisite.'"

"Haruto smiled. 'It always was. You just never noticed before.'"

The Mirror of Death

Guruji let the story settle into silence before speaking again.

"Espen, death is the great mirror that reflects life in its truest form. When we study death, when we reflect on the afterlife, we are not merely pondering what happens when the body turns to dust. We are learning how to live."

"When a man believes he has endless tomorrows, he postpones life. He postpones love. He postpones forgiveness. He tells himself, 'I will chase my dreams someday. I will tell my loved ones I cherish them another time. I will slow down and enjoy the sunrise when life is less busy.'"

"But what if there is no 'someday'?"

He gestured toward the lamps, their golden flames swaying with the wind.

"The moment we remember that life is impermanent, it ceases to be ordinary. A mundane conversation becomes precious. The laughter of a friend, the caress of the wind, the song of a bird—all these small, forgotten things become sacred. Just like the last cup of tea."

Guruji's voice softened, like the fading echo of a temple bell.

"We do not study death to fear it. We study death so that we may finally awaken to life."

Espen lowered his gaze, lost in thought. Around him, the devotees sat motionless, as if afraid to disturb the fragile beauty of the moment.

And somewhere in the distance, a lone nightingale began to sing—its song rising, fleeting, and achingly beautiful, like life itself.

After a long, reflective pause, Guruji gently signalled for a short break. A deep hush lingered in the air, as if the very walls of the hall were absorbing the weight of his words, holding them in sacred stillness. One by one, the devotees rose, moving as if still entranced, their bodies present but their minds drifting through the depths of contemplation.

Some wandered toward the ancient banyan tree, their footsteps slow, deliberate, as if walking through a dream. The massive tree stood like a silent guardian, its gnarled roots twisting through the earth, mirroring the intricate pathways of human thought. Under its vast canopy, a few devotees sat cross-legged on the cool earth, their faces turned upwards as though searching for answers in the labyrinth of branches above.

A little further away, the rich, comforting aroma of freshly brewed coffee and herbal tea intertwined with the crisp morning air. The beverage counter became a quiet refuge—hands wrapping around warm earthen cups, the gentle clinking of clay against wood blending seamlessly with the distant murmur of the wind through the trees. But even here, there was no chatter, no idle talk—only hushed voices carrying the echoes of revelation, as if speaking too loudly might disturb the delicate unravelling of wisdom within them.

Seated on a stone bench beneath the ancient peepul tree, Sujitha, Espen, Kieron, and Astyn sat in silent reverie.

Sujitha, her fingers tracing idle patterns on the damp stone, whispered almost to herself, *"I just can't believe I'm here…"*

There was a tremor in her voice—not of fear, but of awe. The kind that fills the heart when standing at the edge of something vast, something that shifts the very foundation of one's being.

Espen, leaning against the wooden railing nearby, exhaled deeply, his breath carrying the weight of a thousand unspoken thoughts. "The session… it was revealing," he murmured. "So many things we've spent our lives fearing—things that have haunted us, kept us awake at night, things that felt like stones on our chests… now, they don't seem as terrifying. It's like they've been seen for what they are. Shadows… nothing more."

Vasudeva, Padma, Apeksha, and Akshaya simply nodded. No words were needed. Their eyes spoke for them—mirrors reflecting the same silent understanding, the same unravelling of burdens they had carried for so long.

The wind stirred gently, carrying with it the scent of temple jasmine and the distant echoes of a prayer. The soft rustling of leaves blended with the melodic chime of temple bells swaying at the archway, their sound neither abrupt nor intrusive, but rather like an extension of the stillness itself—reminding them that time, like thought, was always in motion.

Just then, Kiran appeared near the threshold of the Buddha Hall. He didn't speak, nor did he need to. His presence alone, his calm, steady gaze, conveyed everything. He lifted a single hand in a quiet gesture.

It's time for the next session.

A shared breath passed between them, invisible yet deeply felt. The devotees slowly rose, some still lost in thought, others gently wiping away silent tears that had escaped unnoticed. Their steps were heavier, yet lighter at the same time—as though the weight of their questions had finally been acknowledged, even if not entirely answered.

As they walked toward the hall, the sky had shifted. The sun, now higher, cast golden streaks through the canopy, illuminating the path ahead. It felt different now—not just a walk toward another discourse, but a journey inward, deeper into the heart of the unknown.

CHAPTER V
Preparing for the Journey Beyond

"Preparing for the journey beyond is not about anticipating an end, but about embracing the unknown with the wisdom of a soul that has lived fully, loved deeply, and learned to let go."

Shree Shambav

Synopsis

This chapter provides practical guidance on how individuals can consciously prepare for the transition beyond physical life. It offers insights into living a life of awareness while embracing spiritual practices that support a peaceful and serene passing. The chapter highlights the importance of regular **meditations**, **rituals**, *and* **affirmations** *to help deepen the connection with the soul, encouraging a state of inner peace and readiness for what lies beyond. Through these practices, individuals can align themselves with their spiritual goals and create an environment of acceptance and harmony. The chapter also emphasizes the value of living consciously, making each moment meaningful, and embracing death not as an end, but as a natural and sacred transition. By* *integrating these spiritual tools and teachings, one can alleviate the fear of death and foster a sense of calm and acceptance when the time comes.*

After a long, contemplative silence, Guruji finally spoke, his voice carrying the weight of a truth long forgotten yet deeply known.

"Preparing for the Journey Beyond," he began, his gaze sweeping over the faces before him, "is not merely about the final moment of leaving this world. It is about how we live now, how we awaken to the truth of our existence, and how we nurture our connection with the eternal."

The devotees leaned in, drawn by the depth of his words.

"Imagine," Guruji continued, "that you are a traveller on a long pilgrimage. You do not wait until the final mile to prepare—you begin long before, gathering provisions, understanding the path, and strengthening your resolve. Death is not an end but a passage, a door through which we walk from one realm into another. And just as a traveller prepares for the road, the wise prepare for their departure with awareness and grace."

Apeksha, her voice quiet yet firm, asked, "Guruji, how do we prepare for this journey? What must we do to ensure a peaceful transition?"

Guruji smiled his expression both tender and knowing.

"Live consciously," he said, *"for the way you live determines the way you leave. If your life is filled with anger, regret, and attachment, your departure will be heavy. But if you cultivate awareness, love, and surrender, then, when the time comes, you will pass like a breeze, effortlessly merging into the vastness."*

He paused, then continued.

"There are three sacred practices to prepare the soul: Awareness, Purification, and Surrender."

1. Awareness: Waking Up from the Illusion

"Imagine a river flowing toward the ocean. The river does not resist; it knows its destination. But a fallen leaf caught in the current may struggle, fearing the vastness ahead. This is how most people live—clinging to their identities, attachments, and fears, forgetting that they are not the leaf but the river itself."

"To prepare for the journey beyond, one must awaken from the illusion of separation. Spend time in self-inquiry. Ask yourself: 'Who am I beyond this body? Beyond my roles and relationships? What remains when all else fades?' Meditate on these questions, and you will begin to taste the truth—that you are not this temporary vessel, but the eternal consciousness that moves through it."

He looked at Vasudeva, whose eyes were brimming with contemplation.

"Practice presence. The more aware you become of each moment, the less fear you will have of losing it. A life well-lived is one where every breath is conscious, where every action is infused with awareness."

2. Purification: Releasing Burdens Before the Final Step

Guruji picked up a handful of sand and slowly let the grains slip through his fingers.

"Each grain is a burden—a regret, an attachment, a wound left unhealed. If you carry them all, how heavy your journey will be. But if you begin to release them now, by the time you reach the threshold of departure, you will be light, ready to soar."

He continued, "Forgive, not for others, but for yourself. Let go of resentment, for it ties the soul to this realm. Speak words of kindness, settle old disputes, and release all that keeps you bound to the past. The purest soul is one that holds nothing, that walks unburdened into the next realm."

Astyn, her voice thick with emotion, whispered, "But Guruji, what if some wounds run too deep?"

Guruji's eyes softened.

"Then take them to the fire of your inner being. Sit in meditation, visualise a sacred flame, and one by one, offer your burdens to it. Say, 'I release this with love. I surrender it to the Divine.' Do this daily, and you will feel the weight dissolve."

3. Surrender: The Art of Merging into the Infinite

The wind stirred, as if carrying his words across unseen dimensions.

"And finally, surrender," Guruji said. "A drop of water clings to the edge of a leaf, trembling in fear of falling. But the moment it lets go, it realises it was never separate from the ocean. This is the truth of the soul—it is never apart from the Divine, only believing itself to be."

"Practice surrender through prayer, through deep trust. Before sleeping each night, whisper to the universe, 'I am yours. Let your will be done.' The more you surrender, the more peaceful your transition will be. When the final moment arrives, you will not fight it—you will step into it as a lover steps into the embrace of the beloved."

The gathering was silent, wrapped in the profound stillness of his words. Even the night seemed to listen.

Guruji closed his eyes for a moment, then softly chanted, *"Om…"* The sacred vibration rippled through the air, settling into their souls like a blessing.

"Prepare, not out of fear, but out of love. Live each moment fully, and when the time comes, step into the great beyond as if stepping into the arms of eternity itself."

Nita rose with folded hands. Her voice was steady, yet carried an underlying depth of yearning. "Guruji, what spiritual practices can help individuals prepare for a peaceful transition at the time of death?"

A hush fell over the hall. The weight of her question rippled through the room, stirring something deep within each soul present.

Guruji closed his eyes for a moment, as if reaching into the unseen realms for an answer beyond words. When he opened them, his gaze was gentle but penetrating.

"Death is not a tragedy, Nita," he began, his voice steady as the earth itself. "It is the final awakening. But what determines whether this transition is peaceful or turbulent is the way we have lived our lives. Death does not arrive suddenly—it has been with us all along, whispering through every fleeting moment, reminding us that all things must pass."

The devotees listened with rapt attention, their hearts stirred by an ancient knowing they had long forgotten.

1. The Art of Awareness: Living with Death as a Companion

Guruji's eyes swept across the hall, his gaze lingering on each seeker.

"Imagine a traveller who knows he must one day leave for a distant land. If he is wise, he prepares his journey well in advance—he does not wait until the last moment to gather provisions. In the same way, if we live with the awareness of our impermanence, we begin preparing for our transition long before our final breath."

A soft murmur rippled through the room, as if this truth had awakened something dormant in their souls.

"Make death your companion, not your enemy," Guruji continued. "Every morning, when you wake, remind yourself: 'This day is a gift. If it were my last, how would I live it?' When you eat, savour each bite as if it were your final meal. When you love, love fully, as if you may not have another chance. When you forgive, do so completely, so you do not carry unfinished burdens into the beyond."

The golden glow of the morning sun illuminated his serene features, making him seem almost ethereal.

2. The Power of Detachment: Releasing the Illusions of Possession

Guruji picked up a single dried leaf that had blown into the hall, twirling it gently between his fingers.

"A river does not mourn the loss of a single drop of water," he said, "because it understands that its essence is not in what it clings to, but in its continuous flow. So too, the soul must learn to release its attachments before the body releases its breath."

The devotees sat motionless, absorbing his words like parched earth, receiving the first drops of rain.

"We spend our lives clutching—holding onto people, to possessions, to identities that we think define us. But nothing here belongs to us. Not even this body. The more we cling, the more difficult the transition becomes. Begin releasing now. Do not wait until your final breath to loosen your grip on the world."

A profound silence followed, the truth of his words settling deep within their hearts.

3. Surrender and Prayer: The Final Offering of the Soul

The temple bells chimed in the distance, as if in affirmation of his next words.

"When a candle's flame flickers for the last time, where does it go?" Guruji asked, his voice barely above a whisper. "Does it die? No—it simply merges with the greater light. The soul is the same. But for this merging to be effortless, one must learn the art of surrender."

He closed his eyes briefly, then continued.

"Surrender does not mean defeat. It means trust. Trust that when the time comes, you are not vanishing into darkness, but returning to the source. The easiest way to cultivate surrender is through prayer. Let each breath be a prayer, each action an offering. Say to the Divine: 'I am yours. Guide me.' When you learn to live in surrender, death is not an interruption—it is a homecoming."

Tears glistened in some eyes, not from fear, but from a deep recognition of the sacredness of the moment.

4. Seva – The Ultimate Preparation for the Journey Beyond

Guruji's voice softened, infused with warmth.

"If you wish for a peaceful death, live a life that brings peace to others. Every act of kindness, every moment of service, is a step toward liberation. Serve not for recognition, but because the light in others is the same as the light within you."

A hush fell over the hall, thick with devotion.

Walking Each Step with Awareness

Guruji let the silence linger, allowing the weight of his words to settle. Then, with a gentle smile, he said:

"If you wish to die well, then live well. Walk lightly, love deeply, and give freely. When the time comes, do not resist—step into the unknown as one who has already made peace with it."

From among the devotees, Vidyarthi slowly rose, his voice steady but carrying the weight of deep yearning. "Guruji, how can meditations, affirmations, or rituals support a deeper connection with the soul?"

A knowing smile graced Guruji's lips, as though he had been expecting this question, as if the universe itself had whispered it into Vidyarthi's heart at the perfect moment. He exhaled softly, letting the silence stretch before he spoke.

The Soul and the Forgotten Language

"Imagine," Guruji began, "that the soul is like a distant friend who once walked beside you, whose voice was once familiar but whom you have long since forgotten. And now, you are trying to remember, trying to call out to them. How do you reconnect? Through language. Through song. Through ritual."

The devotees listened intently, their breathing in harmony with the rhythm of Guruji's words.

"Meditation, affirmations, and rituals are nothing but ways of remembering—whispers sent into the depths of the universe, a call to the forgotten self."

He let his words sink in before continuing.

1. Meditation: The Silence That Reveals

Guruji closed his eyes momentarily, as if stepping into a space beyond the visible world.

"Meditation," he said, "is the language of the soul. It is how we listen when words are no longer enough. Imagine a vast ocean, its surface restless with waves, each wave a thought, an attachment, a fleeting emotion. Most people live on the surface, tossed about by these waves, never knowing the stillness that lies beneath."

"But when you dive deep," Guruji continued, "when you sit in silence and simply observe, you realise something profound: beneath the waves, the ocean is still. The soul is like that depth—unchanging, eternal. Meditation is the practice of diving inward, of sinking past the noise until you reach that silent, boundless expanse where the soul resides."

A gentle breeze swept through the Buddha Hall, carrying with it the fragrance of incense and fresh blossoms. Some devotees closed their eyes, as if already reaching for that depth within.

2. Affirmations: The Echoes That Shape Reality

After a pause, Guruji's voice took on a different rhythm, slow and deliberate.

"Affirmations," he said, "are the seeds we plant in the garden of the mind. Every word you speak, every thought you entertain, shapes the landscape of your reality. If the soul is a divine light, then affirmations are the mirrors we polish so that light may shine without distortion."

He turned toward Vidyarthi with a piercing gaze.

"Tell me, Vidyarthi—if you were to whisper to a child every day, 'You are not enough, you are weak, you will fail,' what would happen to that child's spirit?"

A solemn silence followed. Vidyarthi swallowed, his voice barely above a whisper. "The child would believe it… and become it."

Guruji nodded. "And if you whisper to the soul every day, 'You are divine, you are infinite, you are love itself'? What then?"

A realisation dawned upon the devotees. The room seemed to pulse with an unspoken understanding.

"Affirmations," Guruji continued, "are reminders to the soul of what it already knows but has forgotten. They are the sacred chants, the inner mantras, the seeds of truth we sow until they take root and transform the landscape of our being."

He paused, then spoke softly, as if gifting them a sacred key.

"Begin each day by affirming: 'I am not this body. I am not this mind. I am the eternal soul, untouched, unshaken, and whole.' Say it not just with words, but with knowing."

3. Rituals: The Bridges Between Worlds

The temple bells chimed softly in the distance, marking the movement of time, yet within the Buddha Hall, time felt irrelevant, as if they had stepped into a space beyond it.

"Rituals," Guruji said, "are not mere customs; they are the bridges between the seen and the unseen. Just as a river carves a path through stone over centuries, rituals carve a pathway for the soul to return to itself."

He gestured toward a small **lamp** flickering at the altar, its flame steady despite the gentle breeze.

"Lighting a lamp, bowing before the Divine, chanting sacred names—these are not acts of blind faith. They are echoes of a time when the veil between the physical and the spiritual was thinner. Every ritual, when done with awareness, becomes a doorway, a key that unlocks remembrance."

His voice lowered, almost a whisper.

"The soul does not need rituals, but the mind does. The body does. Rituals are the rhythm of devotion, the dance that allows the formless to take form."

The Final Offering: The Soul's Deepest Longing

Guruji sat in stillness for a long moment, the weight of his words filling the air. Then, in a voice that resonated through the very core of their beings, he said:

"The soul longs for one thing—to return home. Not to a place, but to a state of being, a knowing beyond words. Meditation is how we listen to that longing. Affirmations are how we remember its truth. Rituals are how we honour the journey."

He looked around the hall, meeting each seeker's eyes. "And the ultimate practice?" He paused his next words like the touch of a soft breeze upon a flame.

"To love. To love so deeply that every barrier between you and the Divine dissolves until you realise—you were never separate to begin with."

A profound hush fell over the Buddha Hall. Somewhere, in the quiet distance, the temple bells rang again, their echoes stretching into eternity.

The Art of Living Consciously

Amidst this sacred silence, Vasudeva rose, his voice steady yet carrying a depth of yearning. "Guruji, what practical steps can people take to live more consciously and align with their spiritual goals?"

Guruji looked at him with a gaze that felt both piercing and compassionate, as though he saw not just the question, but the journey that had led to it. He remained quiet for a few moments, allowing the weight of inquiry to settle in the space between them. Then, his voice, rich with wisdom, filled the hall.

The River and the Drifting Leaf

"Imagine," Guruji began, "a river flowing toward the vast ocean. Some leaves, carried by the current, drift aimlessly—tossed about by the waves, unaware of the direction they are moving. But a bird, flying just above, sees the river's path and understands its destination. Most people live like a drifting leaf, unconscious of where life is taking them, reacting to each twist and turn without awareness. But the conscious seeker—he must learn to be like the bird, seeing beyond the immediate, aligning each step with the greater journey."

"Spiritual alignment," Guruji continued, "is not about rejecting the world or escaping life's responsibilities. It is about living each moment with awareness, with a sense of deep participation in the sacred dance of existence. And to do this, one must take practical steps—small but deliberate choices that shape the course of one's life."

Guruji then outlined five essential steps to live consciously and align with one's spiritual purpose.

1. Cultivate Presence: The Art of Being Fully Here

Guruji raised his hand and let it rest in stillness.

"Right now, where is your mind? Is it here, in this hall, fully immersed in this moment? Or is it wandering—thinking of tomorrow, of worries, of things left undone?"

Some devotees shifted uncomfortably, recognising the truth in his words.

"Living consciously begins with presence. Whatever you are doing—whether eating, walking, or speaking—be fully there. When you eat, taste each bite. When you speak, listen deeply. When you sit in silence, truly be in that silence. The past is a memory, the future is uncertain, but the present is the only space where the soul can truly exist. Train yourself to return to this moment, again and again, like a bird returning to its nest."

A hush followed. Some devotees instinctively straightened their posture, grounding themselves in the now.

2. Align Actions with Higher Intentions

Guruji's voice softened but carried a quiet strength.

"Your daily choices shape your spiritual path more than any grand vision or distant goal. Every thought, every action, is either moving you closer to your higher self or pulling you away."

He looked at Vasudeva.

"What is your first thought upon waking? What do you consume—mentally, emotionally, physically? Do your actions reflect the values of your soul, or do they contradict them?"

Vasudeva bowed his head slightly, contemplating the question.

"It is easy to speak of spiritual goals, but real transformation happens in the mundane moments—how you treat a stranger, how you respond to anger, how you hold yourself in adversity. Spiritual alignment is not found in temples alone, but in the kindness you offer, in the patience you cultivate, in the honesty with which you live."

A deep silence settled in the room.

3. Nurture the Mind and Body as a Sacred Vessel

Guruji gestured toward a flickering oil lamp placed at the altar.

"Just as this flame requires oil to burn steadily, your soul requires a healthy body and a pure mind to express itself fully."

He looked around the room.

"How often do you treat your body as a temple? Do you nourish it with care, or do you neglect it? What about the mind—do you feed it with wisdom, or do you let it become cluttered with distractions and noise?"

The devotees sat in deep reflection.

"Practice yoga, eat mindfully, breathe deeply. Protect your mind from unnecessary chaos—limit negativity, surround yourself with uplifting energies. A conscious life begins with the foundation of a strong and clear vessel."

4. Establish a Daily Spiritual Practice

The wind outside carried the faint sound of a distant flute, its melody weaving seamlessly into Guruji's words.

"A seeker without daily spiritual practice is like a traveller without a map. No matter how much wisdom you gather, without daily practice, it remains theory, not experience."

Guruji then suggested practical rituals:

- **Meditation** – "Even five minutes of silent awareness can transform your consciousness."

- **Japa (Chanting Mantras)** – "The vibration of sacred words aligns the mind with higher frequencies."

- **Prayer and Gratitude** – "Begin each day with gratitude, and end it in reflection."

- **Self-Inquiry** – "Ask yourself: 'Who am I beyond this body, beyond this mind?'"

"Even if you begin with just one of these practices, let it be daily. A single drop, consistently falling, can carve through the stone."

5. Surrender and Trust the Flow of Life

Guruji's gaze softened as he spoke.

"A river does not fight the current; it flows with it, trusting that it will reach the ocean. In the same way, surrender is not about passivity—it is about moving with awareness, trusting the intelligence of the Divine."

He turned to Vasudeva with a knowing smile.

"Do not force the path. Do not seek perfection. Walk with sincerity, and trust that each step is taking you exactly where you need to go."

Guruji folded his hands in a silent blessing. The Buddha Hall was thick with the weight of his words, as if the very air had absorbed their meaning.

"A conscious life is not built in a single moment, nor does it require extraordinary acts. It is built in small, deliberate steps—a breath, a choice, a moment of awareness. Walk this path with love, and the Divine will meet you where you are."

A deep stillness followed, and for the first time, Vasudeva felt it—not as an idea, not as a concept, but as a presence within himself.

The Veil Between Worlds: Embracing Death as a Sacred Transition

The Buddha Hall was steeped in a profound silence, the kind that carried the weight of unsaid thoughts and deep contemplation.

Amidst this sacred stillness, Abhilasha rose to her feet. There was a tremor in her voice, not of hesitation, but of a raw, unspoken fear that had lived within her for years. "Guruji, how can embracing the idea of death as a transition help alleviate fear and promote acceptance?"

Guruji remained silent for a long moment, his eyes half-closed as if peering beyond the veil of the material world. Then, he exhaled softly, a knowing smile playing on his lips.

"Abhilasha," he said gently, "what if I told you that death is not the end, but merely a doorway? A passage, not into darkness, but into light unknown?"

The hall remained silent, every heart hanging onto his words.

The Caterpillar and the Butterfly

"Imagine a caterpillar," Guruji continued, his voice flowing like the river outside, steady and full of wisdom. "For its entire existence, it crawls upon the earth, never knowing flight, never knowing the sky. It believes the world to be limited to the leaves it feeds on and the branches it clings to. But one day, a deep stillness takes over—it surrenders to transformation, weaving itself into a cocoon. For the caterpillar, it must feel like the end. A kind of death."

He paused, allowing the image to settle in their minds.

"But then, something miraculous happens. The stillness is not the end; it is the beginning of something greater. The same being that once crawled, now soars. The same creature that feared falling now dances with the wind. The death of the caterpillar was simply the birth of the butterfly."

A hushed awe spread through the hall.

"Death," Guruji said, "is but a cocoon—a moment of transition from one form of existence to another. Just as the butterfly does not mourn the loss of its old self, why should we fear the inevitable transformation of the soul?"

The Fear of the Unknown

Abhilasha's eyes shimmered with unspoken emotion. "But Guruji," she whispered, "why does the idea of death still bring fear?"

Guruji nodded knowingly.

"Fear arises from the unknown. The mind clings to what it understands, and the body fears what it cannot control. But tell me, Abhilasha, do you fear sleep?"

She hesitated, then shook her head. "No, Guruji."

"Why?"

"Because I know I will wake up."

Guruji smiled. "Exactly. The soul does not fear death once it knows it will awaken again. It is only our attachment to this temporary form, this fleeting identity, that makes us tremble at the idea of leaving it behind. But if you deeply understand that you are not the body, not the name, not the story—you will realise that death is not an end, but a return."

The River's Journey to the Ocean

The morning wind stirred the incense smoke, carrying it in spirals toward the high ceiling. Guruji's voice, rich and steady, carried forth another parable.

"A river flows endlessly, winding through valleys and forests, over rocks and through plains, always moving forward. But when it nears the ocean, it hesitates. It fears losing itself. 'What will happen when I merge?' it wonders. 'Will I cease to exist?'"

He let the question linger in the air.

"But the ocean smiles and whispers back, 'You are not losing yourself—you are becoming vast. You are not ending—you are expanding beyond all limits.'"

He turned his gaze to Abhilasha. "This is the truth of the soul. You are not a drop in the ocean; you are the ocean itself in a drop. When the body dissolves, the soul does not perish—it merges back into the infinite. The individual wave disappears, but the water remains eternal."

Practical Steps to Embrace Death as a Transition

A profound stillness filled the hall. Some devotees had silent tears in their eyes—not of grief, but of a newfound clarity. But Guruji knew that wisdom alone was not enough; understanding must be lived, practised, and integrated.

"If you wish to live without fear of death, you must prepare your soul while you are alive."

He then shared three sacred practices to cultivate acceptance:

1. Meditate on Impermanence

"Each morning, before you open your eyes, remind yourself—this day is a gift. This breath is temporary. Everything you see, everything you own, everything you are attached to will one day dissolve. But the witness within you—the awareness—remains."

He gestured toward a flickering oil lamp.

"Just as this flame will burn out, so too will this life. But the light it gave, the warmth it shared—that remains. Let your existence be like this lamp. Live in such a way that when the body fades, your presence remains in the hearts of others, in the love you have shared, in the wisdom you have given."

2. Practice Letting Go

"Most fear of death is fear of loss. We are terrified of losing our loved ones, our identity, our possessions. But the truth is—nothing truly belongs to us. Not even this body."

His gaze swept over the room. "Start small. Let go of anger. Let go of resentment. Let go of the need to control. The more you release, the lighter your soul becomes. The lighter your soul, the easier the transition when the time comes."

3. Remember: You Were Never Born, and You Never Die

Guruji's voice softened to a whisper, yet it echoed with immeasurable depth.

"You are not this body, not this mind. You are the eternal spark—the light that cannot be extinguished. You have lived a thousand lives before this, and you will live a thousand more. But even beyond birth and rebirth, beyond form and name, beyond all cycles—you simply are."

A deep sigh moved through the devotees, as if their very souls were releasing a burden they did not know they carried.

Guruji, his eyes closed for a long moment, breathed in deeply before exhaling—a sound as gentle as the wind rustling through ancient trees. He then turned his gaze toward Abhilasha, his presence as calm as the stillness of a vast ocean.

"Abhilasha," he said, "let me narrate a story."

The King and the Hermit

Once, in a kingdom blessed with abundance and prosperity, there lived a mighty king named Rajan. He was a ruler of great wisdom, but despite all his victories, his heart was troubled. A fear loomed over him—one that no army could defend against, no wealth could bargain with. The fear of death.

Every night, the thought haunted him. "What happens when I die? Will I simply disappear? Will all that I have built crumble to dust?"

He called upon the greatest scholars, priests, and sages of his land, but none could ease his suffering. Some spoke of heaven and hell, others of reincarnation, but their words were only theories. The king wanted truth.

One day, he heard of a hermit who lived deep in the mountains—an enlightened sage said to have conquered the fear of death itself. Determined to find answers, the king set out on a journey, leaving behind his palace, his guards, and all the comforts of his kingdom.

For days, he travelled through thick forests and treacherous paths, until at last, he reached a simple hut by the river. Outside, an old hermit sat in quiet meditation, his presence radiating an inexplicable peace.

The king, accustomed to commanding men, found himself bowing instinctively.

"O Wise One," he said, "I am King Rajan. I have conquered lands, built cities, and ruled wisely. Yet, I tremble at the thought of death. Tell me, how do I prepare for what lies beyond?"

The hermit opened his eyes and smiled; his face lined with years of stillness. "O King, before I answer, may I ask you something?"

The king nodded.

"If a man planned to leave on a long journey, what should he do first?"

The king thought for a moment and replied, "He should prepare—gather food, map his path, and ensure he carries all he needs."

The hermit's smile deepened. "And yet, O King, you know that one day you must leave this world, but you have not prepared for that journey."

The Art of Preparation

The king was silent. The truth of the hermit's words struck him like lightning.

"Then tell me, Sage, how does one prepare?"

The hermit gestured to the river flowing beside them. "Do you see this river? It moves effortlessly toward the ocean, not clinging to the rocks, not fearing the fall of waterfalls. It simply flows."

He then pointed to a withered leaf floating downstream. "But the leaf struggles, fighting against the current, afraid of where it is going. This is the difference between one who is prepared for death and one who is not."

The king listened with rapt attention.

"To prepare for the journey beyond," the hermit continued, "one must first practice letting go. Attachment is the weight that makes the soul fear transition. The more you cling—to your wealth, your power, even your identity—the more painful the passage."

The king lowered his gaze, realising how much he had clung to his crown, his kingdom, his very name.

"What else must I do?" he asked.

The hermit picked up a small lamp, its flame flickering. "Tell me, O King, where does the flame go when the lamp is blown out?"

The king hesitated. "It does not disappear. It merges with the air."

The hermit nodded. "So too does the soul. Death is but the wind that frees the flame from the lamp. If you live with wisdom, compassion, and detachment, your soul will merge peacefully with the Infinite. But if you live with greed, fear, and ignorance, the transition will be one of struggle."

The king's eyes welled with tears. For the first time in his life, death no longer felt like a curse, but a continuation.

Returning Home with New Eyes

After spending many days with the hermit, learning the ways of meditation, self-inquiry, and surrender, the king returned to his kingdom—not as a ruler obsessed with his legacy, but as a seeker who had made peace with the inevitable.

He no longer feared death, for he had begun preparing while he lived. He ruled wisely but without attachment, loved deeply but without possessiveness, and spent time in meditation, aligning with the eternal.

When his final days arrived, he did not resist. He smiled, closed his eyes, and let his soul flow toward the Infinite—like a river returning to the ocean.

The Silence That Followed

Guruji's voice faded into the stillness of the Buddha Hall. No one spoke.

The story had seeped deep into the hearts of the devotees, not as mere words, but as a truth they could feel—a truth that had been waiting to be remembered.

Abhilasha, with tears brimming in her eyes, folded her hands. "Guruji, how do I begin preparing?"

Guruji smiled. "Begin now. Meditate on impermanence, let go of unnecessary burdens, and live with awareness. Remember—when the time comes, it is not an ending, but a return. Just as the river does not fear meeting the ocean, you too will flow home."

The Buddha Hall, once filled with unspoken fear, was now a sanctuary of peace.

Guruji said, "To embrace death is to embrace life. To let go of fear is to finally be free. And to understand the soul's journey is to know—you were never meant to end, only to transform."

The temple bells rang once more, their echoes stretching beyond time, carrying the wisdom into eternity.

Guruji sat in silence for a long. Finally, his voice, both tender and unwavering, broke the hush.

"Let us break for the midday meal."

The devotees slowly rose from their seats, their minds still immersed in the echoes of the morning discourse. Their movements were unhurried, as if reluctant to step away from the sacred stillness of the Buddha Hall. As they walked toward the food canteen, contemplation mingled with hushed conversations, the weight of wisdom settling deep within them.

The aroma of freshly prepared food welcomed them—steaming rice, golden dal, and warm chapatis, served with simplicity and love. The rhythmic clinking of utensils blended with the gentle murmur of voices, creating a symphony of quiet gratitude. Some ate in silence, savouring not just the food but the presence of the moment; others shared reflections from the discourse, their words weaving into the stillness like threads of understanding.

After the meal, some devotees retreated to their shelters, seeking rest in the cool afternoon breeze. Others found solace in the vast embrace of the ashram gardens, their feet brushing against the soft earth, shaded by the ancient trees. A few, drawn by the serenity of the Buddha Hall, returned to sit in stillness, allowing the morning's wisdom to settle within them like ripples dissolving into a still lake.

Beneath the great banyan tree—their sacred meeting place—Akshaya, Nita, Sam, Rohith, and Vasudeva gathered their presence a familiar rhythm in the vastness of the retreat. Soon, Lalitha, Sujitha, Astyn, and Espen joined them, followed by Kiran and Kieron, their arrival adding warmth to the growing circle. Bhavya, Aarna, and Abhirami sat nearby, deeply engrossed in discussing the nuances of the morning session, their voices charged with insight and curiosity. The others listened in quiet reverence, absorbing the wisdom exchanged between them.

Padma, who had been listening intently, turned to Dev, her expression thoughtful.

"Dev, it's time to share your story…" she said gently.

Dev hesitated, his fingers tracing patterns on the dust-covered roots of the banyan tree. A deep breath, a pause. Then, with a voice touched by both nostalgia and vulnerability, he began:

"I was born in the southern part of India. Our family was small but complete—my grandfather, grandmother, father, mother, sister, and me. My father worked for the government, a man of discipline and unwavering principles. My mother was a teacher, diligent in her work, her life devoted to shaping young minds."

He paused, his eyes distant, as if looking through the veil of time.

"My father's discipline was a force we all lived by, and my mother's dedication to education shaped our home. They had high expectations—especially for our studies. My sister was brilliant, always excelling, effortlessly bringing home top grades. I, on the other hand, was different. I loved extracurricular activities and found joy in things beyond textbooks, but my academic performance was… mediocre."

A faint smile crossed his lips, tinged with an old pain.

"I loved my sister, but somewhere along the way, I began to resent her. Not because she was brilliant—but because my parents constantly compared me to her. No matter what I achieved outside of school, my grades always seemed to be the measure of my worth. My mother, despite her love, began pressuring me to study harder, pushing me to spend more hours with my books. Slowly, I began to feel like I wasn't enough. That I was a disappointment."

His voice wavered slightly.

"Even though my sister never boasted, never made me feel lesser, I started to resent her success. I saw in her what I could never be, and instead of admiration, it turned into bitterness. My behaviour changed. I distanced myself from her. My kindness towards her faded into neglect, my words became sharp, my heart heavier with emotions I didn't understand."

The circle around him listened in silence, the weight of his words settling into the afternoon air.

"My father noticed the change before I even understood it myself. One evening, I overheard him telling my mother, 'Do not pressurise him. Let him grow in his own way.' And though my mother tried to ease her expectations, the wound had already been made. No matter how much the pressure lessened, I still couldn't accept my sister's success. It wasn't just about studies anymore—it was about me not being enough."

A deep exhale. His fingers clenched into the earth beneath him.

"And that's when I truly understood—comparison is a slow poison. It doesn't just pit one person against another, it makes you an enemy of yourself. It took me years to unlearn that resentment and to understand that my sister's success was never my failure. That my journey was meant to be my own."

Silence stretched between them, the wind carrying the weight of his story through the rustling leaves.

At that moment, Kiran raised his hand in a quiet signal.

It was time.

The next session with Guruji was about to begin.

One by one, they rose, their hearts heavier yet lighter, filled with thoughts not entirely resolved but deeply acknowledged. As they walked towards the hall, their steps were slower, their presence more rooted—as though something unspoken had been understood.

And in that stillness, in that space of listening and sharing, they knew—they were exactly where they were meant to be.

CHAPTER VI

Unanswered Questions

"The beauty of the infinite lies not in the answers we find, but in the questions that continue to awaken wonder, inviting us to explore deeper realms of mystery and truth."

– Shree Shambav

Synopsis

This chapter explores the profound mystery of the afterlife and existence beyond our physical realm, acknowledging the questions that remain unanswered. It delves into the significance of embracing the unknown, allowing the mystery of life and death to inspire wonder and growth. Faith, curiosity, and awe are celebrated as essential tools in navigating the uncertainty of what lies beyond. The chapter encourages readers to find peace in the unanswered questions surrounding death and to appreciate the beauty and depth of life's mysteries. By fostering a sense of wonder, invited to deepen our connection with the universe, cultivating an attitude of acceptance, gratitude, and reverence for the infinite unknown. Spiritual traditions, combined with personal experiences, offer unique insights, while the journey itself remains an invitation to grow in faith and embrace life's greatest mysteries with an open heart and mind.

Unanswered Questions and the Mystery of the Infinite

Vasudeva, bowed and asked, "Guruji, what truly happens after death? Why do so many great spiritual traditions have different answers? Is there no certainty?"

Guruji's eyes shimmered with a quiet knowing. He let the question settle, as though allowing the very air to breathe it in. Then, in a voice that carried the depth of a thousand lifetimes, he began:

"Vasudeva, come, let us step into the mystery together."

The Blind Men and the Elephant – A Lesson from the Upanishads

"In the ancient Brihadaranyaka Upanishad, there is a parable of blind men and an elephant. A king, wishing to teach a lesson on perception, gathered several blind men and led them to an elephant.

Each man touched a different part. One, feeling the trunk, declared, 'An elephant is like a thick snake.' Another, touching its leg, argued, 'No, it is like a pillar.' A third, feeling its ears, insisted, 'You are both wrong! It is like a great fan.' And so they quarrelled, each clinging to their fragment of truth, none seeing the whole.

So it is with the mystery of the afterlife. Every tradition touches a different part of the Infinite, each grasping a truth, but none fully comprehending its boundless nature."

The hall grew even stiller, the devotees drawn into the gravity of his words.

The Many Paths That Lead to the Ocean

Guruji continued, his voice like a river flowing through the great landscapes of faith.

"In the Bhagavad Gita, Krishna tells Arjuna, '*As a person casts off worn-out garments and wears new ones, so the embodied soul casts off the old body and takes on a new one.*' *(BG 2.22)* Here, the soul's journey is one of continuation, of rebirth, a cycle of experience and evolution."

He paused, letting the sacred verse settle. Then he turned to another path, another doorway into the unknown.

"In **Buddhism**, the Buddha remained silent when asked whether the soul existed after death. Why? Because he knew that clinging to answers traps the mind. Instead, he taught the Anicca, the impermanence of all things. He taught that enlightenment is not about certainty but about awakening from illusion. Nirvana is not a place one travels to after death; it is the extinguishing of false identity, a return to the great Emptiness that is at once fullness."

"In **Christianity**, Jesus spoke of the Kingdom of Heaven, but he also said,

'The Kingdom of God is within you.' (Luke 17:21)

What does this mean? That heaven is not merely a place one reaches after death, but a state of being—a realization of divine presence, here and now."

The devotees listened with rapt attention as Guruji wove together the wisdom of centuries, threading them like pearls on a sacred string.

"In **Sufism**, the great mystic Rumi wrote,

'Don't grieve. Anything you lose comes in another form.'

The Sufis see death not as an end but as a merging with the Beloved, a return to the Source, much like a drop returning to the vast ocean."

He gestured toward the courtyard, where a fountain gurgled, its waters endlessly returning to their origin.

"In **Taoism**, the Tao Te Ching tells us,

'The Tao that can be spoken is not the eternal Tao.' (TTC 1)

That which is beyond life and death cannot be put into words. The wise do not seek answers; they become one with the great unfolding."

A hush settled over the gathering, as though existence itself had momentarily paused.

"In Jainism, Mahavira taught that karma binds the soul, and liberation comes from shedding all attachment. The soul, purified of all bondage, ascends to a realm beyond time."

Guruji folded his hands, his expression serene. "So, Vasudeva, do you see? The paths may be different, but all lead to the Infinite."

The Beauty of Not Knowing

Vasudeva, deep in thought, finally spoke. "But Guruji… if we do not know the full truth, how do we live with the uncertainty?"

Guruji smiled, his eyes shining with a quiet joy.

"Uncertainty, my child, is the gateway to wonder."

Guruji said, "Consider a child standing by the ocean for the first time. Does he demand to know where the waves come from, where they go? No—he runs into them, laughing, feeling their rhythm, dancing with their mystery.

In the same way, life is to be lived—not as a puzzle to be solved, but as a vast ocean to be experienced."

A soft sigh rippled through the hall, a collective exhale, as though a great burden had lifted.

Faith, Curiosity, and the Path Forward

Guruji's voice softened, "So, do not fear the unanswered questions. Do not fear the Infinite. Instead, *live with curiosity. Live with reverence. Live with faith.*

If the great mystery calls you, sit in silence - 'Meditate, Pray, Love deeply'. Let go of your attachments. Let go of the need for absolute certainty."

And when the time comes, when you stand at the threshold of the beyond, you will not tremble. *"You will smile, You will bow, You will step forward, not into darkness, but into a light greater than you have ever known."*

The devotees sat in absolute silence.

Embracing the Unanswered: The Art of Surrendering to the Unknown

Aastha, her brow furrowed in quiet contemplation. Her voice, though soft, carried the weight of deep yearning. "Guruji, how can we find peace in accepting the unanswered questions surrounding death and the afterlife?"

Guruji's eyes, in a voice that carried the depth of centuries, he began:

The Parable of the Two Birds

"In the **Mundaka Upanishad**, there is a beautiful parable of two birds perched on the same tree.

One bird, the lower one, hops from branch to branch, pecking at the fruit—sometimes sweet, sometimes bitter. It is restless, hungry, always searching, never satisfied. The other bird, higher up, watches silently, untouched by craving, radiant in its stillness.

This lower bird, dear one, represents the restless mind—forever seeking answers, forever grasping at the fruits of knowledge, forever troubled by the questions of the unknown. But the higher bird… it simply observes. It does not chase certainty, nor does it fear mystery. It just is."

Guruji looked at Aastha, his gaze gentle yet piercing. **"Which bird will you choose to be?"**

Aastha swallowed, her fingers curling around the edge of her shawl. The question was not one of knowledge but of surrender.

The River That Surrenders to the Ocean

He continued his voice like the steady flow of a river.

"In **Taoism**, Lao Tzu teaches us that the greatest wisdom is to flow with the current, not against it. The river does not resist its journey to the ocean. It does not question what awaits it beyond the horizon. It simply flows, trusting that its destination is not an end, but a becoming."

He gestured towards the small stream that ran through the ashram gardens, its waters meandering towards an unseen destination.

"Why do we fear the unanswered?" he asked. "Because we wish to control the current. We fear being the river that does not know the shape of the ocean it will merge into. But true peace comes not from knowing—but from trusting."

The Candle and the Infinite Light

A soft breeze stirred the temple bells, their chime merging with the murmur of the devotees' breath.

"In **Sufism**, Rumi speaks of the candle and the eternal flame. Imagine a small candle, flickering in the darkness. It fears the wind, it fears the night, it fears being extinguished. But then—"Guruji paused, his fingers forming a delicate flame, "—it is touched by the great, eternal Light.

And in that moment, it realises it was never meant to remain separate. The little flame does not die—it becomes part of something vast, something limitless."

He smiled. "So too, with us. Death is not the snuffing out of a candle—it is the merging with the Infinite."

Aastha's eyes shimmered with something unspoken, something raw yet comforting.

The Space Between the Notes

Guruji took a deep breath, his gaze sweeping across the silent seekers before him.

"In music, what gives a melody its beauty? It is not just the notes—but the spaces between them.

Imagine a great symphony, flowing like a river of sound. Now, if one were to remove the silence, if one were to demand that every space be filled with sound—would it still be music?

No. It would be noise. Chaos."

He folded his hands. *"Life, too, has its spaces of silence— its unanswered questions, its mysteries, its unknowns. They are not mistakes. They are the spaces that give meaning to the melody."*

And so, dear one, do not seek to fill every silence. *"Let some mysteries remain. Let some questions breathe. Let the Infinite remain infinite."*

Aastha exhaled, as though releasing something she had unknowingly held for too long.

Living the Questions

Guruji closed his eyes for a moment, as though listening to something beyond words. Then, he spoke once more.

"In the end, we must learn to live the questions, rather than demand the answers.

Rainer Maria Rilke once wrote:

"Be patient toward all that is unsolved in your heart and try to love the questions themselves, like locked rooms and like books that are written in a foreign tongue… The point is to live everything. Live the questions now. Perhaps you will then gradually, without noticing it, live along some distant day into the answer."

Guruji smiled, his voice barely above a whisper now. "So let us walk our path not with the need for certainty, but with the grace of wonder. Let us trust like the river trusts the ocean. Let us surrender, like the candle surrenders to the light. Let us embrace the spaces between the notes."

And when our time comes, when the Great Unknown calls us forward, let us not tremble. Let us smile, let us bow… and let us step into the mystery, not with fear, but with love."

The temple bells rang once more—soft, distant, eternal.

And in the silence that followed, Aastha found something she had not been searching for—**peace.**

Faith, Wonder, and Curiosity: The Sacred Dance with the Unknown

The devotees sat in deep contemplation, their breaths slow, their minds filled with the weight of the teachings imparted thus far. It was in this sacred pause that Kiran, his voice filled with sincerity and a quiet yearning, asked: *"Guruji, what role do faith, wonder, and curiosity play in embracing the mysteries of existence?"*

A smile flickered across Guruji's lips—gentle, knowing, as if he had been waiting for this very question. He closed his eyes for a moment, as if listening to the whispers of something unseen.

The Parable of the Child and the Star

"Many years ago," Guruji began, "there was a little boy who lived in a small village at the foot of a great mountain. Every night, he would sit by his window and gaze at the stars, his eyes wide with wonder. One star, in particular, captivated him—a brilliant, shimmering light that seemed to call to him across the vast expanse.

One evening, he asked his grandfather, 'What is that star? What lies beyond it?'

The old man smiled and said, 'That, my child, is a mystery.'

The boy frowned. 'But I want to know! I want to see it up close!'

His grandfather placed a hand on his head and said, 'Then let your wonder guide you. Let your curiosity be your feet, your faith be your compass, and your heart be your lantern. One day, you may not reach that star, but you will have travelled far beyond what you ever imagined.'"

Guruji paused, looking at Kiran.

"And so, this is the essence of our journey. Faith, wonder, and curiosity—they are not separate things. They are the three sacred wings upon which the soul soars toward the Infinite."

Faith: The Unseen Bridge Over the Abyss

He leaned forward slightly, his eyes deep pools of knowing.

"Faith is like a bridge over a great abyss. It allows us to walk forward, even when we cannot see the other side.

In **Hinduism**, faith is called **Shraddha**—not blind belief, but an inner conviction that the unseen is as real as the seen. Arjuna, in the Bhagavad Gita, stood on the battlefield, paralyzed by doubt. But Krishna did not give him mere knowledge—he gave him faith. And that faith became the chariot that carried him forward.

So too in **Christianity**, when Peter saw Christ walking upon the water, he stepped forward in faith. But the moment doubt clouded his heart, he began to sink. *Faith is the thread that connects the finite to the Infinite. It is the bridge that allows us to walk where reason fears to tread."*

Guruji's gaze swept across the hall, the weight of his words settling into the hearts of those listening.

Wonder: The Gateway to the Divine

He took a deep breath, his voice softening, as though recalling a forgotten song.

In **Sufism**, Rumi speaks of the intoxication of divine wonder—of how the lover of God does not seek answers but dances in awe of the Beloved.

Wonder is the child within us who never stops asking 'Why?' It is the wide-eyed gaze that sees the divine in a blade of grass, in the laughter of a stranger, in the vastness of the cosmos.

Taoism teaches us that the wise do not claim to know—they simply marvel at the unfolding mystery. Lao Tzu tells us that the Tao which can be spoken is not the eternal Tao, for the moment we think we have grasped it, it slips through our fingers like water.

Guruji said, "When we lose our sense of wonder, we reduce existence to mere explanations. But life is not something to be explained—it is something to be experienced. *A sunset is not beautiful because we understand its science. It is beautiful because it stirs something beyond words within us.*"

He chuckled softly. "The sages say that God hides in plain sight—not in temples alone, but in the rustling of leaves, in the dance of fireflies, in the hush before dawn. *And only those who have the eyes of wonder can see Him.*"

Curiosity: The Fire That Keeps the Soul Alive

Guruji's voice grew steady again, like the steady rhythm of an eternal drum.

"Curiosity is the courage to step into the unknown. It is what led **Siddhartha Gautama** to leave his palace in search of truth. It is what led the mystics, the seers, the explorers of every age to walk beyond the edges of certainty.

In **Jainism**, Mahavira spoke of **Anekantavada**—the idea that truth has many sides, and we must keep seeking, keep questioning, and never settling for a single answer.

In **Islam**, the Quran asks, *'Do they not travel through the land, so that their hearts may learn wisdom?'* To seek, to question, to journey—this is the sacred duty of the soul.

But, the greatest curiosity is not about the stars above, nor the oceans beyond. The greatest curiosity is this— **Who am I?**

And when this question truly burns within us, we begin the real journey—not outward, but inward. That is when faith, wonder, and curiosity cease to be mere concepts… and become the breath of the soul itself."

The Mystery is Not to be Solved, But Lived

Guruji exhaled softly, the weight of his words merging with the stillness of the hall.

"You ask how to embrace the mysteries of existence?" He smiled, looking at Kiran.

"Do not seek to conquer the mystery—fall in love with it."

Stand before it not with fear, but with reverence. Walk with faith, knowing that the path will reveal itself.

Carry wonder in your heart, for that is where the divine speaks. And never let your curiosity dim, for it is the eternal flame that will guide you home.

And one day, when your time comes, may you step into the Infinite—not with hesitation, not with answers, but with the simple, profound joy of a traveller who has walked the path with open eyes and an open heart."

The Ocean and the Drop: A Journey into the Infinite

Sam, his voice carrying both longing and hesitation, finally spoke. "Guruji, how do spiritual traditions and personal experiences contribute to our understanding of the infinite?"

"Sam," Guruji began, "let me tell you a story. There was once a small drop of water that had fallen from the sky into a great ocean. For the longest time, this drop believed itself to be separate—an individual, small and vulnerable. It feared being lost, dissolved, forgotten."

"But one day, the drop encountered a wise sage sitting by the shore. The sage whispered, 'You are not separate. You are the ocean itself, only in a different form.' The drop, bewildered, asked, 'But how can I be the ocean? I am so small, and it is so vast.' The sage simply smiled and said, 'Dive into yourself, and you will know.'"

Guruji paused, his gaze sweeping across the seekers. "This is the essence of all spiritual traditions, Sam. They are the sages sitting by the shore, whispering to the drop that it is, in truth, the ocean."

The Wisdom of Traditions: Many Paths, One Truth

Throughout history, spiritual traditions have served as pathways guiding seekers toward the ultimate reality—the bridge between the finite self and the infinite essence of existence. While their expressions may differ, their core truth remains the same: the soul's journey is one of awakening, of remembering its divine nature. Each tradition offers a unique lens through which to view this great mystery, yet all converge upon the realisation that beyond the illusions of separation, there is unity.

Hinduism: The Recognition of the Self as Divine

Hinduism describes the infinite as **Brahman**, the ultimate, formless, all-pervading reality. According to the **Upanishads**, this eternal truth is not something external to be attained, but rather the very essence of our being. The phrase **Tat Tvam Asi**—"You are That"—reminds the seeker that the **Atman** (individual soul) is not separate from Brahman, but rather an expression of it. **Moksha**, or liberation, is attained when one transcends the illusion of separateness (**maya**) and realises their oneness with the Absolute.

A river, upon reaching the ocean, no longer maintains its identity as a river—it becomes the vast, endless sea. Likewise, when the soul awakens to its true nature, it dissolves into the boundless expanse of Brahman, free from all limitations.

Buddhism: The Path to Emptiness and Infinite Potential

Buddhism approaches the infinite through the lens of **nirvana**, the extinguishing of the false sense of self. The Buddha taught that suffering arises from attachment to an illusory identity. Through meditation, wisdom, and ethical living, one realises that the self is merely a collection of changing phenomena, much like a wave upon the ocean—impermanent and without independent existence.

At the heart of this teaching is **shunyata**—emptiness—not as a void, but as infinite potential. Just as a sky free of clouds reveals the vastness of space, the mind, free from egoic illusions, becomes boundless, open, and luminous. Nirvana is not annihilation but absolute liberation—a state of profound peace, beyond birth and death.

Christianity: Surrendering to Divine Union

In Christianity, the infinite is understood as God, the source and sustainer of all things. The path is one of surrender—letting go of personal will and aligning with divine grace. Jesus spoke of this union when he said,

"I and the Father are one." (John 10:30).

The contemplative traditions of Christianity emphasise silence, prayer, and inner stillness as the means to divine communion.

"Be still, and know that I am God." (Psalm 46:10).

Here, "knowing" is not intellectual but experiential—an immersion in the divine presence. The Christian mystics, like St. John of the Cross and Meister Eckhart, describe this as the *dark night of the soul*, where the individual self dissolves into the infinite love of God, much like a drop merging into the ocean.

Sufism: Love as the Bridge to the Infinite

Sufism, the mystical path of Islam, sees the infinite as the Beloved—God, the source of all love and beauty. The soul is likened to a lover yearning for reunion with the divine. Rumi, the great Sufi poet, wrote:

"You were born with wings, why prefer to crawl through life?"

The Sufi seeks annihilation of the ego (**fana**) in order to become one with the divine essence (**baqa**). This dissolution is not death but true life—the realisation that the soul was never separate from its source. The great Sufi saints, such as Al-Hallaj and Rabia, expressed this through ecstatic poetry, music, and dance, seeing every breath, every moment, as an opportunity to dissolve into the infinite embrace of the Divine.

Taoism: Flowing with the Infinite

In Taoism, the infinite is known as the **Tao**—the Way, the formless source of all things. Unlike traditions that seek to grasp or define the infinite, Taoism teaches **wu wei**—effortless action—flowing in harmony with existence rather than resisting it.

The **Tao Te Ching** states: *"The Tao that can be spoken is not the eternal Tao."* This means that the ultimate truth is beyond words and concepts; it must be experienced directly, like a river that surrenders to the flow without resistance. Just as water naturally finds its way to the ocean, the soul, when free of attachments, effortlessly aligns with the infinite rhythm of the universe.

Jainism: The Illumination of the Soul

Jainism describes the infinite as **Kevala Jnana**—pure, infinite knowledge. Unlike theistic traditions, Jainism teaches that the soul itself is inherently divine, but it is weighed down by karma, much like a mirror covered in dust. Through rigorous self-discipline, meditation, and non-violence (**ahimsa**), the soul gradually sheds its impurities, revealing its boundless, luminous nature.

The Jain concept of liberation (**moksha**) is a return to the soul's original state—free from birth, death, and suffering, shining with infinite perception and bliss. It is the ultimate state of self-realisation, where one transcends all limitations and merges with the eternal flow of existence.

One Truth, Many Reflections

Each of these traditions offers a different door to the same truth. Like many rivers flowing into the same ocean, they point toward the same realisation: that beyond the illusion of separateness, there is only unity.

- Hinduism shows the infinite as **Brahman**, the unchanging reality.

- Buddhism reveals it through **nirvana**, the extinguishing of the illusion of self.

- Christianity finds it in **divine union**, surrendering to God's love.

- Sufism experiences it as **ecstatic love**, dissolving in the Beloved.

- Taoism flows with it through the **Tao**, embracing the effortless way of existence.
- Jainism attains it by purifying the **soul**, revealing its boundless knowledge.

Like a diamond reflecting light from different angles, each tradition offers a facet of the same eternal mystery. The infinite is not something distant to be reached—it is here, now, within us. The journey is not about going anywhere, but about awakening to the truth that has always been.

Guruji looked around the hall, his gaze deep yet gentle. "No single path holds the entire truth, yet each one holds a part of it. Honour the wisdom of the traditions, but do not let them become barriers. The infinite is not bound by names or concepts—it is lived, felt, and ultimately realised in the silent depths of the soul."

The Key to Understanding

"But traditions alone are not enough," Guruji continued his voice a soothing river. "They can guide you, but the journey must be walked by you alone. Personal experience is what turns knowledge into wisdom."

- The monk who sits in meditation for years does not merely believe in peace—he becomes peace.

- The devotee who surrenders in prayer does not just imagine God's presence—she feels it within.
- The artist who loses himself in the moment of creation touches something beyond time.
- The mother who gazes into her child's eyes knows the love that cannot be measured and cannot be contained.

"Every moment where you dissolve into something greater than yourself—whether through love, suffering, silence, or devotion—is a glimpse into the infinite."

Sam listened, his heart opening like the petals of a long-forgotten flower.

"So tell me, Sam," Guruji asked, "is the drop truly separate from the ocean?"

Tears welled in Sam's eyes. He had no words, only a deep knowing—a feeling that transcended thought.

Guruji smiled again, ever so gently. "Do not seek the infinite as though it were far away. It is not in the heavens alone, nor ancient scriptures alone. It is here, now, within you. Let go of the illusion of separateness, and you will find that you were never lost."

The Beauty of the Unknown: A Journey into Awe and Gratitude

Abhirami's voice carried a quiet reverence. "Guruji, in what ways can the beauty of the unknown inspire gratitude and awe in our daily lives?"

Guruji, seated in serene contemplation, let the question settle in the stillness of the space. After a moment, his voice was gentle yet profound. "Abhirami, let me tell you a story."

The Monk and the Ocean of Stars

Long ago, in the heart of the Himalayas, there lived a monk named Raghavan. He had dedicated his life to the pursuit of knowledge, seeking answers to life's greatest mysteries. He studied the scriptures, meditated for days at a time, and contemplated the vastness of existence. Yet, despite all his wisdom, a quiet restlessness remained within him. He wanted certainty—he longed to grasp the ultimate truth, to understand the divine completely.

One evening, as he sat on a mountaintop, he looked up at the vast expanse of the night sky. The stars stretched endlessly before him, shimmering like celestial jewels scattered across an infinite canvas. He gazed at them for hours, his heart swelling with both wonder and frustration.

"What is this universe?" he whispered. "Why am I here? What lies beyond all that I can see?"

At that moment, an old sage appeared beside him. His eyes were filled with the depth of a thousand lifetimes.

"Why do you seek to contain the infinite within the limits of your mind?" the sage asked.

Raghavan was silent.

The sage continued, "Does the ocean lose its beauty because you cannot see its depths? Do the stars stop shining because you do not know their names? Must a bird understand the wind to soar across the sky?"

Raghavan listened, his heart trembling.

"The unknown is not meant to be feared," the sage said, "but to be loved, to be embraced, to be lived."

At that moment, Raghavan understood. The beauty of life was not in having all the answers—it was in the sheer miracle of existence itself. The vastness of the universe was not a puzzle to be solved, but a mystery to be celebrated. The monk fell to his knees, tears of gratitude streaming down his face. The same sky that once filled him with frustration now filled him with awe.

The Sacredness of the Unseen

Guruji paused, his eyes searching the faces before him.

"Abhirami, the unknown is not an absence of knowledge—it is the presence of infinite possibilities. When we look at a sunrise, do we demand to understand every colour of the sky before we admire its beauty? When we hold the hand of a loved one, do we need to know the chemistry of emotions before we feel love? Life is woven with mystery, and in that mystery lies its greatest gift."

Guruji said, "Hinduism speaks of Brahman, the vast, formless reality beyond comprehension. Buddhism teaches us to embrace the impermanence of all things, surrendering to the flow of existence. Christianity speaks of faith—that we may not always see, but we must trust in divine wisdom. Sufism teaches that the lover need not know the Beloved's plan, only that love itself is enough."

He smiled, his voice filled with warmth.

"When we allow ourselves to be humbled by the unknown, we cultivate awe. And where there is awe, there is gratitude."

Finding Wonder in Everyday Life

He turned back to Abhirami.

"So how can we let the unknown inspire gratitude and awe in our daily lives?"

1. **By seeing each day as a gift:** The fact that we wake up each morning is a miracle. The breath flowing in and out of our lungs, the unseen forces keeping our hearts beating—these are mysteries beyond our understanding, yet they sustain us. Should we not bow in gratitude for this simple, profound blessing?

2. **By embracing uncertainty as part of the journey:** Imagine a book where you already knew the ending. Would you still turn its pages with excitement? Life, too, is a story unfolding moment by moment. When we stop demanding certainty, we open ourselves to the magic of the unexpected.

3. **By looking at nature with reverence:** A single flower blooming from the cracks of a stone holds a universe of wisdom. The waves of the ocean, moving endlessly yet never questioning their path, teach us how to trust the rhythm of existence. In nature, we find the poetry of the infinite.

4. **By practising silence and stillness:** When we quiet our minds, we begin to hear the whispers of the unknown. In the stillness of

meditation, in the spaces between our thoughts, we touch something greater than ourselves. The unknown does not reveal itself through force, but through surrender.

5. **By realising that love itself is an enigma:** Why do we love? What makes the presence of another soul stir something indescribable within us? Love is the greatest mystery of all, yet it is also the most real thing we will ever know. Should we not live in awe of this boundless force that connects us?

The Infinite Within

Guruji leaned back, his eyes shining with a quiet radiance.

"Abhirami, the unknown is not outside of you—it is within you. You are part of this grand mystery, just as the stars, the rivers, and the winds are. Instead of seeking to conquer the unknown, dance with it. Instead of fearing what lies beyond, open your heart to wonder. And in doing so, every moment of your life will become sacred."

Silence filled the hall, but it was not empty—it was rich with the weight of understanding. The devotees sat still, their hearts echoing with the truth of Guruji's words. Some closed their eyes, breathing in the enormity of the lesson. Others gazed beyond the windows, as if seeing the world for the first time.

Abhirami pressed her palms together in deep reverence. "Guruji, I see it now. The unknown is not something to be solved—it is something to be lived with devotion."

Guruji nodded, a gentle smile playing on his lips. "Yes. And in living it fully, you will find that gratitude and awe are not destinations—they are the path itself."

After a long pause, Guruji exhaled gently, his voice carrying the weight of the moment. "Let us take a break."

Outside the Buddha Hall, a soft drizzle fell, weaving silver threads through the darkened sky. The scent of wet earth mingled with the delicate fragrance of blooming jasmine, a quiet symphony of nature. The air was cool, and crisp, whispering with the hush of raindrops kissing the leaves.

After a brief reprieve, warmed by steaming chai and crisp evening snacks, a small group of devotees gathered under a modest shelter near Brindavan Garden. The twilight sky stretched in hues of deep indigo, the first stars shyly peeking through the thinning veil of clouds. The rhythmic patter of rain on the roof filled the silence between them, a space heavy with thought and unspoken reflection.

Sam, who had been staring into the distance, finally turned to Dev. His voice was quiet, expectant. "Dev… what happened next?"

Dev took a slow breath, his eyes clouded with memories. The past, though distant, still lived within him, etched into the fabric of his being.

"I changed," he began, his voice heavy. "Not for the better."

The words hung in the air before he continued.

"I became arrogant. My bitterness grew like a slow poison, infecting everything. Every little mistake my sister made became an excuse for me to lash out. I had started hating her—openly, unapologetically. And yet… she continued to love me, without conditions, without resentment."

He let out a hollow chuckle, shaking his head. "It was almost unbearable, that love."

He paused, gathering himself before continuing.

"One day, my father took me to a meadow near our home. The grass swayed gently in the evening breeze, the sky painted with hues of dying sunlight. He placed a hand on my shoulder and said, 'Dev, you are the elder one. The way you treat your sister… it's not right. She loves you deeply, yet you push her away. Try to be kind to her.'"

Dev's jaw tightened at the memory. "I snapped. His words irritated me. I yelled, 'Are you saying I am bad?'"

He looked away, his fingers curling into fists as if bracing against the past.

My father's voice was calm, and patient. *'No, Dev. I am saying that sometimes we fail to see love when it stands right in front of us.'*

"But I wasn't willing to listen. I felt like no one understood me. I accused him of favouring her, of loving her more just because she was good at academics. I let my resentment blind me. No matter how much he tried to make me understand, I refused."

The night deepened around them, the rain softening into a whisper. Dev's voice, too, became quieter, as if he was finally stepping into a wound he had long ignored.

"Days passed. I buried myself in my own world, refusing to let anyone in. Then, during my high school years, I won a trophy in badminton. For the first time, I felt proud. I saw admiration in my parents' eyes. I felt seen."

A faint, fleeting smile crossed his lips, but it vanished as quickly as it came.

"That evening, my sister came home from school, and my mother, beaming with pride, told her about my achievement. My sister's face lit up with joy. She rushed to see the trophy and lifted it in her hands like it was something sacred. But then…"

He swallowed hard, the weight of the memory pressing against him.

"It slipped."

The words were barely above a whisper.

"The glass trophy shattered on the floor."

His hands clenched. The pain in his voice was no longer about the trophy—it was about everything it had come to represent.

"I was furious. Blinded by rage. Without thinking, I hit her. Hard. She stumbled, and in the chaos, I pushed her—so hard that her head banged against the wall. She collapsed."

A sharp inhale cut through the group. The rain outside had stopped, but the storm within Dev's voice had not.

"She fell unconscious. Blood trickled from her head. My father rushed her to the hospital. Four stitches."

His breath was shaky now. "Four stitches… but it could have been worse. It could have been something unforgivable."

The silence that followed was unbearable. Dev's voice, now hollow, carried the weight of regret.

"My father didn't say a word to me that day. Not one. My mother didn't scold me. And my sister… my sister stopped talking to me. Even when my father insisted she forgive me, she wouldn't."

He exhaled sharply. *"And yet, I still didn't feel I had done anything wrong. I convinced myself that she had broken my trophy on purpose. That she deserved my anger."*

The group sat frozen in the stillness of the night, the weight of his story pressing against their hearts.

In the distance, the temple bell rang—a soft, resonant chime, calling them back.

Kiran signalled silently. "It was time."

One by one, they rose, but Dev lingered, his gaze lost in the past. As they made their way back.

SECTION THREE

A Reflection

"In the silence of the unknown, we find the echo of our deepest questions—each unanswered mystery is not a void, but an invitation to explore, to expand, and to grow into a deeper connection with the infinite."

-Shree Shambav

CHAPTER VII
Embracing the Eternal

"To embrace the eternal is to surrender to the timeless flow of existence, where the boundaries of life and death dissolve, and we realise that we are both part of the vastness and the stillness that precedes and follows every breath."

– Shree Shambav

Synopsis

In this chapter, we explore the profound philosophical and spiritual reflections on death, the afterlife, and the eternal nature of existence. By embracing these concepts, we can enrich our human experience, finding deeper meaning in every moment. The chapter encourages us to reflect on the nature of eternity and how it shapes our understanding of life, death, and the soul's journey. Through insights drawn from various philosophical and spiritual perspectives, we discuss how the awareness of our impermanence can inspire a more purposeful, fulfilled, and mindful existence. Embracing the eternal is not just a theoretical exercise, but a practical guide for navigating the challenges of daily life with a sense of deeper connection to something greater than ourselves.

Embracing the Eternal:

Roopa sat with quiet anticipation, her heart carrying a question that had long dwelled in the deepest chambers of her soul. "Guruji," she began softly, "what does it truly mean to embrace the eternal? How can reflecting on death and the afterlife deepen our experience of living?"

Guruji closed his eyes briefly, then opened them with a serene smile. "Roopa, let me tell you a story."

The Wise Potter and the Clay Vessel

There was once a wise potter who lived in a quiet village by the river. With his aged hands, he shaped the earth into vessels of breathtaking beauty. Each morning, he would sit before his wheel, moulding the soft clay with patience, whispering prayers as he worked. His pots were admired far and wide, yet he never seemed attached to any of them.

One day, a young disciple, filled with admiration but also confusion, asked, "Master, you pour so much love into creating these vessels, yet you do not grieve when they break. How is that so?"

The potter smiled and placed a freshly shaped pot in the disciple's hands.

"My child," he said, "this clay was once formless earth, resting beneath our feet. Today, it takes the shape of a vessel. One day, it will return to the dust it came from. But does its journey make it any less beautiful?"

The disciple stared at the pot, his mind awakening.

"Everything in this world," the potter continued, "is like this vessel. Our bodies, our possessions, even the people we love—everything arises, serves its purpose, and dissolves. If I were to weep for a broken pot, would it not be like weeping for the setting sun?"

Guruji paused, letting the weight of the story settle. Then he continued, his voice carrying the wisdom of the ages.

"Roopa, life is like that clay vessel. It is given form for a time, and then it returns to the great formlessness from which it came. But instead of seeing this as a loss, we must see it as a sacred transformation."

The Dance Between Life and Death

Across traditions, the great mystics and sages have spoken of this eternal truth:

- In Hinduism, death is not an end, but a doorway. The Bhagavad Gita proclaims: *"Just as a person discards old clothes and wears new ones, so too does the soul discard its old body and take on a new one."* (Bhagavad Gita 2:22) Death is merely the soul stepping from one room into another.

- In Buddhism, impermanence (anicca) is the fundamental nature of all things. To resist it is to suffer; to embrace it is to attain freedom. The Buddha taught: *"All conditioned things are impermanent. When one sees this with wisdom, one becomes disenchanted with suffering."*

- In Christianity, death is not a separation, but a homecoming. Jesus said, *"In my Father's house, there are many rooms... I go to prepare a place for you."* (John 14:2) Love does not die; it transcends.

- In Sufism, the soul's longing for the Divine is like a river flowing into the ocean. Rumi wrote, *"When the soul leaves the body, it is like a bird escaping from its cage, finally free to soar."*

- In Taoism, life and death are two sides of the same flowing river, inseparable. Laozi taught: *"To be born is to emerge; to die is to return. Both are part of the great Tao."*

- In Jainism, true liberation (moksha) comes when the soul sheds its karmic burden and merges with its pure, infinite state. Death is not feared but seen as the dissolving of illusion.

How Embracing Death Enriches Life

Guruji turned his gaze towards Roopa, his eyes filled with knowing.

"When we live with the awareness of death, life itself becomes sacred. Every sunrise is no longer just a sunrise—it is a miracle. Every moment with a loved one is no longer mundane—it is a divine gift. Every breath is no longer unnoticed—it is grace itself."

He gestured to the trees outside, their leaves trembling in the morning wind.

"Look at that tree, Roopa. It does not fear autumn when its leaves must fall. It knows that in letting go, it makes space for spring to return. Should we not learn from the trees? Should we not live in full bloom while we are here, and when the time comes, surrender gracefully to the eternal?"

The hall was silent, but it was not emptiness—it was full, as though each person had touched something vast within themselves.

Practical Ways to Embrace the Eternal

1. Live as if each moment is a farewell.

Not in sadness, but in gratitude. Tell those you love what they mean to you. Do not waste time in anger, resentment, or delay. If you were to leave this world tomorrow, how would you spend today?

2. Meditate on impermanence.
Reflect on the transient nature of all things. The flower that blooms will wither, and the waves that rise will return to the ocean. When we stop clinging to what is temporary, we open ourselves to what is eternal.

3. Cultivate inner peace.

Do not wait until death to seek the infinite—begin now. Through prayer, meditation, and self-inquiry, touch the divine within you. As the Upanishads say: *"That which is immortal is already within you."*

4. Surrender to the mystery.

Some things will never be answered, and that is the beauty of it. The universe is a grand, infinite tapestry—why demand to see every thread when you can marvel at the whole?

The Eternal Awakening

Guruji's voice softened as he concluded.

"Roopa, embracing the eternal does not mean waiting for death. It means waking up to the fullness of life, right now. When we stop resisting, we realise that death is not the opposite of life—it is a part of it, woven into its fabric like night into day."

A single tear glistened in Roopa's eye, but it was not of sadness. It was of recognition.

"Guruji, I understand now," she whispered. "To embrace death is to embrace life fully."

Guruji smiled. "Yes. And in that embrace, you will find that what you seek—the eternal—has been within you all along."

Padma her eyes held the quiet intensity of a seeker, one whose heart was burdened with profound contemplation. "Guruji," she asked softly, "how can embracing the concept of eternity influence our perception of life, death, and the afterlife?"

Guruji looked at her with infinite tenderness, as though he had already seen the shape of her question forming in the vastness of time. He let the silence stretch, allowing the gravity of the inquiry to settle into the hearts of all present. "Padma, to understand eternity, let me tell you a story."

In a quiet valley nestled between snow-capped peaks, there was a river unlike any other. The people of the land called it **Ananta**, meaning "endless," for though they had traced its course for generations, no one had ever found its source, nor had they ever seen where it disappeared into the horizon.

The river was ancient, flowing long before the village had been built, and it would continue long after the last footprints faded from its banks. The villagers revered it, whispering prayers into its waters, for they believed it held the wisdom of all those who had ever lived.

One day, a young seeker named Arjun stood at the river's edge, troubled by questions of existence. He had witnessed birth and death, joy and suffering, yet he could not reconcile the fleeting nature of life with the vastness he felt within his soul.

Turning to the river, he asked, *"O wise one, tell me—where do you begin, and where do you end?"*

The river only laughed, its ripples shimmering in the sunlight.

"I do not begin, nor do I end," it murmured. *"I have taken many forms—once, I was a mist rising from the mountains, then a stream rushing through the forest, and now, I am a river flowing toward the sea. But even when I reach the ocean, I do not cease to exist. I simply become something else."*

Arjun's heart stirred.

"Then what of those who have gone before us?" he asked. *"Where are they now?"*

The river swirled around his feet like a gentle embrace.

"They are here, within me. They have always been here."

A deep silence settled within Arjun. He closed his eyes, and in that moment, he understood: Life, death, and the afterlife were not separate—they were different ripples of the same endless current.

The Ocean of Eternity:

Guruji's gaze swept across the hall, the weight of the story settling over the listeners like a warm, unseen presence.

"Padma, just as the river does not grieve when it reaches the ocean, we too must understand that life and death are not opposites. They are part of the same eternal movement."

The Wisdom of Traditions: Many Paths, One Truth

Throughout human history, spiritual traditions have sought to bridge the gap between the finite and the infinite. While they use different languages, symbols, and metaphors, they ultimately point to the same fundamental truth—that life and death are not opposites but part of a greater, eternal existence. Each tradition provides a unique lens through which we can understand eternity, offering wisdom that transcends time and culture.

Hinduism: Brahman—The Infinite and Unchanging Reality

Hinduism speaks of Brahman, the supreme, formless, and infinite reality that pervades all existence. Unlike the transient world, which is subject to birth and death, Brahman is unchanging, eternal, and absolute.

The Bhagavad Gita (2:12) declares:

na tvevaham jaatu naasam na tvam neme janaadhipah|
na chaiva na bhavishyaamah sarve vayamatah param||

Meaning: "Never was there a time when I did not exist, nor you, nor all these kings; nor in the future shall any of us cease to be."

This verse reveals the eternal nature of the soul (Atman), which is neither born nor does it die. Just as waves rise and fall in the vast ocean without ever being separate from it, life is a temporary manifestation of the eternal Brahman. Death is merely a return to the source, much like a river flowing back into the sea.

The Upanishads, the philosophical texts of Hinduism, express this idea in the great Mahavakya (great saying) Tat Tvam Asi—"You are That." This profound statement teaches that the individual self (Atman) is not separate from the infinite reality (Brahman). Enlightenment (moksha) is realising this unity and transcending the illusion of separation.

Know Thyself: The Eternal Inquiry

On the gate of the temple of Apollo at Delphi are inscribed the words, Gnothi Seuton, or "Know Thyself." This ancient injunction, simple yet profound, has echoed through centuries, challenging seekers to look beyond the surface of their identities and inquire into the nature of the self.

Guruji smiled and said, "Socrates was fond of encouraging people to ask this very question. There is a story—perhaps a legend—about him."

Once, Socrates was walking through the streets of Athens, lost in deep contemplation. His eyes were distant, his mind navigating the vast landscapes of thought. In his reverie, he accidentally bumped into a passerby, who irritated, turned and exclaimed,

"Can't you see where you're going? Who are you?"

Socrates, momentarily pulled from his inner world, looked at the man and chuckled, replying,

"My dear fellow, I have been pondering over that question for the last forty years. If you ever come to know who I am, please let me know."

The man scoffed and walked away, but those who stood nearby, students and philosophers alike, saw the profound truth in Socrates' words. The question "Who am I?" is not one to be answered easily. It is not a matter of name, profession, or lineage, but an inquiry into the very essence of existence.

Adi Shankaracharya and Shiva: The Question of the Self

Guruji's eyes gleamed as he continued, "A similar conversation is said to have taken place between Adi Shankaracharya and Lord Shiva."

It is told that once, as the young Adi Shankaracharya was walking towards the temple of Kashi, he encountered an old man standing in the middle of a narrow path. The man, appearing as an untouchable, was blocking Shankaracharya's way.

Shankaracharya, believing in the traditional customs of his time, asked the man to move aside so that he could pass. But instead of stepping aside, the old man smiled and asked,

"O revered one, whom do you wish to move—this body or the soul?"

Shankaracharya was taken aback.

The old man continued, "If you wish the body to move, then remember that the body is only matter, composed of the five elements. Can matter move matter? If you wish the soul to move, then tell me—where should it go? The soul is infinite, omnipresent, beyond movement. So, tell me, O wise one, whom do you wish to move?"

Shankaracharya stood still, realisation dawning upon him. He fell at the old man's feet, recognising that this was no ordinary being but Shiva himself, testing him.

Shiva smiled and said, "Know thyself, O Shankara. You are neither the body nor the mind. You are the eternal self, the unchanging consciousness."

It is from such encounters that Adi Shankaracharya later composed his great works on Advaita Vedanta, declaring:

"Chidananda Rupa Shivoham Shivoham"

(I am pure consciousness, I am Shiva, I am Shiva.)

The Great Inquiry: Who Am I?

Whether it is Socrates inquiring into the nature of the self, or Adi Shankaracharya encountering Shiva's profound wisdom, the question remains the same:

Who am I?

Am I this body that will one day perish? Am I this mind that changes like the wind? Or am I something beyond—something eternal, formless, boundless?

All spiritual traditions urge us to turn inward. The Bhagavad Gita says:

"The wise do not mourn for the living or the dead, for the soul is eternal, beyond birth and death."

The Upanishads declare:

"That which sees but cannot be seen, hears but cannot be heard—That is the Self, the immortal, the unchanging reality."

The Buddha taught:

"There is no self in the way the world thinks. But beyond this illusion of self, there is pure awareness, vast as the sky."

In Christianity, Jesus said:

"The Kingdom of God is within you."

Thus, the question is not merely philosophical—it is the very key to liberation.

Guruji looked at the gathering and said, "To know oneself is not to add more layers of identity, but to strip them away until only truth remains."

"Know Thyself" is not just a commandment carved in stone; it is an invitation—a lifelong pilgrimage into the depths of our own being. And when we finally discover the answer, we realize that we were never separate from it."

Buddhism: The Realisation of Timelessness

Buddhism approaches eternity differently—not as a linear timeline, but as the realisation that time itself is an illusion. The Buddha taught that all things are impermanent (Anicca), and what we perceive as birth and death are simply changes in form, not absolute beginnings or endings.

He said:

"Nothing ever truly arises, and nothing ever truly ceases."

This teaching is deeply connected to Shunyata (emptiness), which means that all things lack an independent, fixed existence. To perceive eternity is to go beyond the illusion of self and time, experiencing the ever-present now.

In Zen Buddhism, this is often explained through meditation, where a person experiences the stillness beyond thoughts, realising that liberation (nirvana) is not a place but a state of being completely present in the eternal now.

The Diamond Sutra states:

"Past mind cannot be grasped, present mind cannot be grasped, future mind cannot be grasped."

The awakened being no longer clings to the past or future but abides in the realisation of timeless existence.

Christianity: Eternal Life as Union with the Divine

Christianity teaches that eternity is not merely about living beyond death, but about union with God, a relationship that transcends time. Jesus said:

"Whoever believes in me has eternal life." (John 6:47)

Here, eternal life is not just a continuation of existence, but an intimate, unbreakable connection to the Divine.

The soul, much like a drop of water, is never truly separate from the infinite love of God.

Christian mystics, such as Meister Eckhart, often spoke of eternity as being fully absorbed in God's presence, where human identity dissolves into divine unity. The Apostle Paul echoes this idea in Romans 8:38-39:

"Neither death nor life...nor anything else in all creation will be able to separate us from the love of God."

Thus, in Christianity, eternity is not measured in time but in the depth of connection with the Divine—a love that knows no boundaries.

Sufism: The Dance of Annihilation and Eternal Love

Sufism, the mystical branch of Islam, sees life and death as part of a divine dance. The goal of the soul is Fana (annihilation of the ego) and Baqa (eternal existence in God).

The great Sufi poet Rumi wrote:

"When the soul leaves the body, it is like a caged bird finally set free to soar in the endless sky."

For the Sufi, death is not an end but the final surrender into love itself, like a drop merging into the ocean. The soul has always belonged to the Divine, and death is simply a return to that beloved state.

Another famous Sufi verse describes this beautifully:

"Don't cry when I die, for I am not leaving—I am returning home."

For the Sufi, eternity is not about survival but about becoming one with divine love, much like a moth consumed by the flame of truth.

Taoism: Flowing with the Eternal Tao

Taoism teaches that the infinite is not something to be grasped, but something to be flowed with. The Tao (the Way) is both the source and the destination—life and death are simply shifts within its unfolding.

Laozi, the founder of Taoism, wrote in the Tao Te Ching:

"To know the eternal is to be enlightened."

This wisdom suggests that those who resist change suffer, while those who flow with the natural rhythm of existence find peace. Just as seasons change effortlessly, life and death are not disruptions but transitions within the grand harmony of existence.

A Taoist sage would look at a river and understand:

- Life is the river's flow.
- Death is the river reaching the ocean.

- But the river was never separate from the ocean to begin with.

To know eternity in Taoism is to let go of control and trust the natural unfolding of existence.

Jainism: Liberation Through Pure Knowledge

Jainism describes eternity in terms of the soul's liberation from karma. Every soul is eternal, but it remains trapped in cycles of birth and death due to its attachments and actions (karma).

The ultimate goal is Kevala Jnana (pure infinite knowledge), a state where the soul is freed from all bondage and exists in its pure, blissful nature, beyond time and space.

Mahavira, the 24th Tirthankara of Jainism, said:

"The soul is eternal. It is neither born nor does it die. Only its journey changes."

Thus, death is not an end, but a release into pure awareness. The liberated soul, like the unclouded sun, shines with infinite clarity and peace.

The One Truth Behind Many Paths

While these traditions offer different perspectives, they all point to the same fundamental truth:

- Life and death are not opposites but part of the same eternal cycle.
- The soul is never truly separate from the infinite.
- Fear of death arises from illusion, and wisdom dissolves that fear.

Like the river that eventually merges with the sea, each of us is on a journey home—whether we call it Brahman, Nirvana, God, the Tao, or Pure Awareness.

The wise do not cling to the transient but live with deep reverence for the eternal, knowing that even in the smallest moment, the infinite is present.

And so, as Rumi said:

"You were born with wings. Why prefer to crawl through life? Lose yourself to find yourself."

Living with Eternity in Our Hearts

Guruji's voice softened, drawing the wisdom inward.

"Padma, when we embrace eternity, we no longer live in fear of endings. We begin to live with reverence, knowing that every moment is sacred."

1. See life as a passage, not a destination.
If we live believing we are only this body, only this fleeting identity, we will fear death. But if we see ourselves as travellers—souls on an infinite journey—then each moment becomes a sacred step toward greater understanding.

2. Love without attachment.
Do not hold onto people, possessions, or experiences as if they are permanent. Love them deeply, but freely—knowing that they, like the river, will change and flow into something new.

3. Find eternity in the present.
Do not wait for an afterlife to touch the infinite. It is here, in this very breath, in the stillness between thoughts, in the eyes of a loved one. As the Taoists say: *"Eternity is not in the future, it is in the depth of now."*

4. Trust the unfolding.
The caterpillar does not mourn its end—it surrenders to transformation, knowing that the butterfly is already within it. Likewise, we must trust that death is not a loss, but a transition into something vast and beautiful.

The Silent Understanding

Padma sat motionless, her breath slow, as though something vast had just unfolded within her.

"Guruji," she whispered, "I think I understand now. We are not separate from eternity. We have always been part of it."

Guruji smiled, "Yes, Padma. The river does not fear where it is going, for it knows—it is already home."

The Wisdom of Impermanence:

Apeksha asked, "Guruji, in what ways can reflecting on death and the soul's journey lead to a deeper sense of purpose and fulfilment?"

A hush settled over the Buddha Hall as Apeksha's question hung in the air, deep and profound.

Guruji closed his eyes for a moment, as if listening to something beyond the veil of ordinary perception. Then, with a serene smile, he spoke. "Apeksha, let me share a story."

The King and the Yogi

Long ago, in a vast and prosperous kingdom, there lived a mighty king. He had everything one could wish for—power, wealth, family, and prestige. Yet, despite his abundance, a shadow loomed over him, an invisible fear gnawing at the edges of his happiness.

One day, he summoned a revered yogi to his court and said, "I have conquered lands, ruled justly, and surrounded myself with every pleasure. Yet, I am troubled. No matter how much I achieve, I live with a fear that nothing lasts. I wake in the night, restless, knowing that one day, all this will slip through my fingers. Tell me, wise one, how can I find peace?"

The yogi looked at the king with deep compassion and said, "Your fear is not of loss—it is the fear of forgetting who you truly are."

The king furrowed his brows. "What do you mean?"

The yogi gestured toward the palace garden, where a magnificent lotus pond stretched before them. "Tell me, my king, which is more real—the water or the lotus?"

The king frowned. "The water, of course. Without it, the lotus cannot exist."

The yogi nodded. "And yet, do you grieve when the lotus withers at the end of the season?"

The king hesitated. "No, because I know that the pond remains, and in time, new lotuses will bloom."

The yogi smiled. "Just as the pond remains when the lotus fades, so too does your true self remain when this body dissolves. Your soul is not the passing bloom of this temporary life—it is the eternal water, deep and boundless."

The king sat in stunned silence. For the first time, he saw his life not as a desperate attempt to cling to fleeting pleasures, but as a journey—a sacred unfolding.

From that day onward, he ruled with a new awareness. He cherished each moment, not with fear of losing it, but with gratitude for having lived it. And when his final hour arrived, he met it not with dread, but with the peace of one who knows that the river does not end when it meets the sea.

The Gift of Mortality

Guruji paused, allowing the story to sink in before continuing.

"Why do we fear death, Apeksha? Because we believe it is the end of our story. But what if, instead of an ending, it is merely a transition? The soul, like the lotus, rises from the waters of existence again and again. And when we understand this, something incredible happens—we begin to live fully."

In Hinduism, the Bhagavad Gita tells us:

"Never was there a time when you nor I did not exist, nor will there be a time when we cease to be." (Bhagavad Gita 2:12)

This realisation does not make life meaningless—on the contrary, it makes every moment sacred. When we know that we are passing travellers in this world, we stop taking our days for granted. We speak kinder words, love without hesitation, and forgive more easily. We become more present because we understand that this present moment is all we truly have.

The Soul's Journey: Learning Through the Veil of Time

Buddhism teaches that everything is impermanent—**Anicca**. The Buddha once said:

"The problem is, you think you have time."

And yet, in this impermanence lies great beauty. Imagine if the sky remained the same colour forever, if the seasons never changed, if music had no ending—would we still cherish their beauty? It is the fleeting nature of a sunset that makes it breathtaking. It is the knowledge that our time is limited that urges us to live meaningfully.

Sufism embraces this truth with deep love. **Rumi** wrote:

"Be like a traveller in this world. Let the road be your home, and let your heart carry no burden but love."

The **Tao Te Ching** teaches that the river never mourns the loss of a drop, because it understands that the drop was never separate from the whole. Life and death are not opposites; they are simply two aspects of the same eternal flow.

In Christianity, Jesus said:

"Whoever believes in me has eternal life." (John 6:47)

Faith, in its purest form, is the understanding that we are already eternal. The body may fade, but love, wisdom, and the essence of our being continue.

Living With Purpose, Dying Without Regret

Guruji looked around the hall. Some had tears in their eyes, others sat in deep contemplation.

"Reflecting on death does not lead to despair—it leads to clarity. It frees us from petty worries and reminds us of what truly

matters. We stop wasting time on things that do not nourish the soul. We let go of grudges, not because we must, but because we realise they weigh us down. We express love without hesitation. We serve others, knowing that in doing so, we serve the Divine within them."

He continued, his voice gentle yet powerful:

"If you were told that you had only one year left to live, how would you live? Would you not make peace with those you have wronged? Would you not wake up every morning with gratitude? Would you not cherish the laughter of your loved ones a little more?"

A deep silence filled the Buddha Hall. Apeksha wiped a tear from her cheek.

Guruji smiled. "This is how we must live every day."

And then, with a voice full of warmth and certainty, he said:

"The greatest gift of reflecting on death is that it teaches us how to live."

Navigating Life's Challenges Through the Lens of the Infinite

Akshaya, folded his hands and asked, "Guruji, how do philosophical and spiritual perspectives on the eternal help us navigate the challenges of daily life?"

Guruji looked at him for a moment, his expression both serene and knowing. He leaned slightly forward, his voice gentle yet profound. "Akshaya, imagine a man lost at sea."

The Sailor and the North Star

There was once a sailor who set out on a great voyage across the ocean. He was strong, determined, and skilled, but as the days passed, the weather turned treacherous. Towering waves rose against his fragile boat, and dark clouds swallowed the sky. He struggled against the forces of nature, trying desperately to navigate his course, but the storm was merciless.

For hours, then days, he fought against the elements. He was exhausted, battered, and close to surrender. And then, suddenly, the clouds parted just enough for him to glimpse the North Star.

With renewed determination, he fixed his gaze upon it. He could not control the waves, nor could he stop the wind, but as long as he had that one guiding light, he knew which direction to steer. He surrendered to the rhythm of the ocean, not in despair, but in trust. Instead of resisting the storm, he flowed with it—knowing that as long as he kept his eyes on the eternal, he would find his way.

The Anchor of the Infinite

Guruji paused, letting the imagery settle before continuing.

"Life is like that ocean, Akshaya. Some days, it is calm, and we sail smoothly. Other days, the storm comes—grief, failure, uncertainty, and loss. When we look only at the waves, we feel helpless. But when we fix our gaze upon something eternal—whether it is God, truth, dharma, or the wisdom of the soul—we are no longer lost."

In Hinduism, the Bhagavad Gita Chapter 2, Verse 27 reminds us that we are not these fleeting identities but the eternal self.

jaatasya hi dhruvo mrityur dhruvam janma mritasya cha|

tasmaad aparihaarye 'rthe na tvam shochitum arhasi||

Meaning: "That which is born must die, and that which dies must be born again. But the soul is neither born nor does it ever die."

When we understand this, the struggles of daily life lose their power to shake us. We work, we love, we strive—but we do not cling.

Buddhism echoes this wisdom, teaching that suffering comes from attachment to what is temporary. The Buddha said,

"Nothing is permanent. Everything arises and passes away. To be at peace, we must see this clearly."

When we embrace this truth, we stop resisting life's changes and instead learn to flow with them, much like the sailor who surrendered to the sea while keeping his eyes on the North Star.

The Eternal in Daily Life

Akshaya's eyes were fixed on Guruji, absorbing every word.

"But Guruji, how do we apply this wisdom in our everyday struggles?" he asked.

Guruji smiled. "Consider a man facing financial ruin. If he believes his worth is tied to wealth, he will be devastated. But if he sees himself as part of something larger—if he understands that circumstances change but the soul remains untouched—he will find the strength to rebuild."

He continued, his voice filled with quiet conviction.

"Or take a person who loses a loved one. Grief will come, as it must. But if they understand that love does not die, that the soul transcends this world, their sorrow will be tempered with faith. They will mourn, yes, but they will not be broken."

Christianity teaches this same truth. Jesus said:

"Do not store up for yourselves treasures on earth, where moth and rust destroy, but store up treasures in heaven." (Matthew 6:19-20)

What are these heavenly treasures? *Love. Wisdom. Kindness. The courage to live truthfully.* These are eternal. When we anchor ourselves in these, life's storms may shake us, but they will not sink us.

Sufism and the Art of Letting Go

Guruji's eyes twinkled as he recalled a story from the Sufi tradition.

"A Sufi master once said, 'Live in this world as a guest in an inn. Enjoy the food, rest in comfort, but do not cling—for soon, you must depart.'"

Akshaya smiled faintly, sensing the wisdom in the words.

"When we accept that everything is temporary—success, failure, pain, joy—we stop trying to control the uncontrollable. Instead, we focus on living well, with sincerity and gratitude. We do our best, but we do not despair when things do not go our way."

This is the essence of Taoism as well. **Laozi wrote:**

"To hold on too tightly is to invite suffering. The wise one flows like water, moving effortlessly around obstacles."

The river does not resist the rocks in its path—it flows around them. Likewise, when we see our struggles in the light of the infinite, we do not resist life—we move with it.

Walk with the Eternal

Guruji's voice softened. "Akshaya, when we align ourselves with the eternal, we no longer live in fear. We work hard, but we are not slaves to success. We love deeply, but we do not cling. We face hardship, but we do not collapse under its weight. We walk through life with grace, because we know that we are more than these fleeting moments—we are the infinite itself."

The hall was silent, the only sound was the rustling of leaves outside. Akshaya sat back, his heart lighter, his mind clearer.

He had come seeking answers for life's struggles. And in Guruji's words, he had found something greater—a way to live without fear, with wisdom as his North Star and eternity as his guide.

The Art of Living with Impermanence

Akanksh, a young seeker with searching eyes, folded his hands and asked, "Guruji, what practical steps can we take to integrate the awareness of life's impermanence into a more meaningful and mindful existence?"

Guruji smiled, his eyes radiating warmth. He let the question settle into the silence before speaking, his voice carrying both gentleness and depth. "Akanksh, imagine a man standing on the banks of a great river."

The River and the Raft

There was once a traveller who came to the edge of a mighty river. On one side was the world he had known—his village, his loved ones, his familiar comforts. But beyond the river lay something unknown, a land he longed to reach.

The current was swift, and he knew he could not cross by swimming alone. So, he built a sturdy raft, tying logs together with care. As he stepped onto it, he felt gratitude—this raft would carry him across, keep him afloat amidst the shifting waters.

But when he reached the other shore, he hesitated. The raft had been so useful, so protective—should he carry it on his back, just in case he needed it again?

It seemed absurd, and yet, is that not what we do in life? We cling to what once served us—identities, possessions, grudges, fears—forgetting that they were only meant to help us cross a particular phase. The wise traveller, realising this, bowed to the raft, thanked it, and left it behind.

He stepped onto new land, unburdened and free.

The First Step: Letting Go of the Unnecessary

Guruji turned to Akanksh. "This is the first step, Learn to let go."

Hinduism speaks of Anitya, the transient nature of all things. In the Bhagavad Gita (2:14), Krishna tells Arjuna:

maatra-sparshaas tu kaunteya shitoshna-sukha-duhkha-daah |

agamaapayino 'nityas tans-titikshasva bharata | |

Meaning: "O son of Kunti, the interaction between the senses and their objects gives rise to fleeting experiences of pleasure and pain. These sensations are temporary, arising and fading like the changing seasons of summer and winter. O descendant of Bharata, learn to endure them with equanimity, without being disturbed, for they do not define the eternal self."

Guruji said, "Just as winter and summer come and go, so too do pleasure and pain. Bear them with patience, knowing they are temporary."

We suffer not because things change, but because we resist their changing.

So, how do we practice letting go?

Reflect on what you are clinging to:

Is it an old hurt? A rigid expectation? A fear of the future?

Acknowledge that everything is temporary:

Relationships evolve, success wanes, and even the body ages—fighting it only brings suffering.

Practice non-attachment, not indifference:

Love deeply, but do not possess. Work hard, but do not be enslaved by ambition. Enjoy life's gifts, but do not build your identity around them.

Buddhism teaches the same in its concept of **Anicca**, or impermanence. The Buddha said,

"Nothing ever remains as it is. When you accept this, you stop grasping at illusions and begin to live freely."

The Second Step: Living Fully in the Present

Guruji's voice softened as he continued.

"If life is impermanent, then every moment is precious. This is the second step: Be fully present."

Too often, we live as if we are merely passing through, waiting for the "real" life to begin after we achieve something—after the promotion, after the marriage, after retirement. But the only real life is happening now.

Christianity echoes this in Matthew 6:34:

"Do not worry about tomorrow, for tomorrow will worry about itself. Each day has enough trouble of its own."

How can we cultivate presence?

- **Mindful Breathing:** Throughout the day, pause. Take a deep breath. Feel it enter and leave your body. This breath is a reminder—you are alive, here, now.
- **Savour Ordinary Moments:** The warmth of tea in your hands, the laughter of a child, the

rustling of leaves—these are life's hidden treasures.
- **Limit Regrets and Worries:** The past is gone. The future is uncertain. But this moment? This is yours to live.

Sufism expresses this beautifully. Rumi wrote:

"Be like a child, utterly immersed in the moment, dancing in the rain, laughing without reason. That is how you touch eternity."

The Third Step: Serve with Love

Guruji's gaze swept across the hall:

"And finally, Akanksh, if life is impermanent, then what we do with it matters deeply. This is the third step: Use your fleeting time well."

Jainism speaks of Seva, selfless service, as a path to liberation. Kevala Jnana, or pure knowledge, is attained not merely by knowing truth but by embodying it through kindness.

Cultivate compassion: If everything and everyone is impermanent, then every interaction is sacred. A kind word today may be the last you speak to someone.

Give without expectation: True giving comes not from obligation, but from abundance. The Tao Te Ching says:

"The sage gives without keeping score, for in giving, he receives everything."

Live in alignment with your values: When you understand that your days are numbered, you stop wasting time on trivial pursuits. You act with courage, and love without holding back, and forgive more easily.

The Fourth Step: Live as the Sky, Not the Cloud

The hall was silent now, the weight of Guruji's words sinking in. He let the quiet stretch before offering one final reflection.

"Akanksh, the sky does not mourn when the clouds pass—it knows they were never permanent. Be like the sky. Let thoughts, fears, joys, and sorrows come and go, but do not mistake them for who you are."

The Upanishads speak of this wisdom:

"You are not the body, not the mind, but the eternal Self. The witness, unchanging, beyond birth and death."

When you live with this understanding, impermanence is no longer a source of fear—it becomes your greatest teacher.

- You love more, because you know everything is fleeting.

- You suffer less, because you do not cling to what must pass.
- You live fully, because you see life as a gift, not a burden.

Guruji smiled, his eyes reflecting a deep, timeless knowing.

"So, do not fear the impermanence of life. Let it awaken you. Let it make you more alive. Let it teach you how to love, how to serve, and how to surrender to the great mystery with gratitude in your heart."

Akanksh bowed deeply. He had come with a question about impermanence—but he left with the wisdom of how to truly live.

WRAP UP

A Journey Through Life After Death

A Stillness Beyond Words

After a gentle pause, Guruji closed his eyes, his serene face radiating a stillness so profound that it seemed to echo the very essence of his teachings. The hall fell into a reverent silence, as if the very air had stilled in devotion. It was a silence that was not empty, but full—a silence that spoke of wisdom, of understanding, of truths too deep for words.

His presence, unshaken and eternal, was more eloquent than any discourse. It was the presence of one who had gone beyond, who had seen through the illusions of the world and rested in the unshakable peace of the Self. And in that moment, the devotees felt it—not just heard or understood, but felt the stillness he carried within him, as if they, too, had touched the very heart of truth.

With a soft, knowing smile, Guruji rose from his asana with effortless grace. Every movement carried an air of purpose, as though he embodied the stillness he had imparted. Without a word, he turned and began to walk toward the exit, his white robes flowing behind him like a silent hymn to the sacred art of presence.

A Reflection on the Journey

For a long moment, no one moved. The devotees remained seated in quiet communion, their breaths slow and deliberate, their thoughts weaving through the tapestry of wisdom Guruji had just shared.

The once-bustling Shambav Hall now felt transformed—a sanctuary imbued with Guruji's presence, each corner glowing with the light of understanding and the weight of introspection.

The retreat had reached its final evening. And yet, for many, it felt like the true journey had only just begun.

A Shared Awakening

Later that night, after a simple but fulfilling meal, a small group gathered around the fireplace outside. The fire crackled softly, casting golden embers into the cool night air, each spark rising like a fleeting prayer before dissolving into the vast darkness. The sky stretched above them, an infinite canvas adorned with a thousand shimmering stars. Fireflies flitted between the trees, their soft glow flickering in rhythm with the nocturnal symphony—the distant croaking of frogs, the whispering of leaves, the gentle trickle of a nearby stream.

Nature, in all its quiet grandeur, was awake.

Among those gathered were Akshaya, Padma, Dev, and Vasudeva, their faces illuminated by the shifting glow of the fire. Nearby, Nita, Sujitha, Espen, and Astyn sat in deep discussion, their voices carrying the echoes of Guruji's teachings. The night held them all in its embrace, binding them in shared reflection.

Akshatha was the first to speak, her voice quiet, yet weighted with emotion.

"This retreat has been an awakening. A mirror to our deepest selves."

The others nodded in agreement.

Padma, her voice rich with the wisdom of lived experience, added, "Guruji's teachings always reveal new dimensions—of life, of love, of the unseen ties that bind us."

Apeksha, after a moment of silence, murmured, "'Communicating with the Departed' touched something deep within me. There were questions I had carried for years… and today, they found their answers."

Vasudeva's gaze softened, his voice carrying the weight of memory. "'The Soul's Ultimate Destination'… That session brought back my parents. I lost them so young, and yet today, I felt as though I spoke to them again. My journey with Guruji was accidental… but looking back, I see it was never an accident. It was fate. A lifeline."

Padma's eyes welled with tears. Akshaya, Kiran, and Vidyarthi instinctively reached out, their silent comfort speaking more than words ever could.

After a long pause, John turned to Dev, curiosity flickering in his eyes. "Dev… what happened next?"

Dev's Story: A Bridge Between the Past and the Present

The firelight cast dancing shadows on Dev's face as he took a deep breath, his gaze lost on the shifting embers. The past had never truly left him—it had only been waiting, lingering in the quiet spaces of his soul, asking to be seen.

"Days turned into years," he began, his voice steady but heavy. "The distance between me and my sister grew, not just physically, but emotionally. Even though my parents insisted she speak to me, she refused. She was afraid of me."

A sharp exhale. A brief silence.

"But my ego... my cursed ego... it wouldn't let me bridge that distance."

The words landed heavily, their truth undeniable.

"I completed my engineering. I moved to Singapore. I built a life, a career, a name for myself. I stayed away for more than ten years, and when I finally returned to India to start my own business... the distance between me and my sister had hardened into a wall. A wall I had built with my own hands."

A hush fell over the group. The fire crackled, filling the silence.

"One day, by accident, I found my sister's old diary."

His voice faltered for a moment. He swallowed hard.

"I opened it. And what I read... shattered me."

A deep breath. A flicker of pain in his eyes.

"Page after page, I saw the love she had held for me. The admiration. The longing. Even when I had pushed her away, even when I had given her every reason to hate me… she had only loved me. To her, I had been a hero. A protector. A brother she had always believed in, even when I had failed her over and over again."

A slow exhale. The weight of a lifetime in a single breath.

"I could not sleep for days. The shame consumed me."

His voice turned softer.

"One night, I went to my mother and said, 'I am ashamed of what I have done. I was cruel to you. To Father. To my sister. I don't deserve forgiveness.'"

His mother's reply had been simple, yet profound.

"She smiled and said, 'We have already forgotten, my child. Why do you still remember?'"

A pause. A shift in the air.

"I went to my father next. I apologised. He held my hand and said, 'Dev… we are family.'"

The fire crackled, mirroring the emotions flickering across the listeners' faces.

"And then… my father asked the question that shattered me completely."

He swallowed hard.

"'Did you speak to your sister?'"

The silence that followed was unbearable.

"I lowered my head. I had no words. Only tears."

He ran a hand over his face as if wiping away the years.

"I wanted to. But I was afraid. How could I undo the past?"

"And then… fate led me to Guruji."

His eyes softened, the memory vivid.

"It was at one of his retreats. As I sat listening to his discourse, something within me broke. I wept like a child. I had carried the weight of my ego for too long."

He took a deep breath.

"After the session, Guruji called me."

"He asked me, 'What burdens your heart?'"

"I told him everything."

"And Guruji simply smiled and said, 'Call her. She is waiting.'"

A tremor in his voice. A pause. A heartbeat.

"That evening, I did."

His voice broke.

"The moment she answered, she cried. And she asked me only one thing… 'Brother, why did it take you so many years to call me? Did I do something so unforgivable?'"

Tears welled in his eyes.

"I could only say… 'No. I was a fool. And I am sorry.'"

The wind sighed through the trees, carrying the unspoken prayers of the night.

The devotees sat in silence, their souls heavy with emotion.

Above them, the stars shimmered.

The fire whispered.

And somewhere, deep within, they knew—the retreat had ended. But their journey had only just begun.

Life Coach and Philanthropist

Shree Shambav is the visionary founder of the Shree Shambav Ayur Rakshita Foundation (www.shambav-ayurrakshita.org). He founded this institution with a lofty goal: to recognise human identity across gender, ethnicity, and nationality. Through this organisation, he wants to assist all communities in realising their full potential and the intrinsic beauty of life.

Shree Shambav, a Life Coach, is dedicated to supporting people on their journeys of self-discovery and empowerment. He assists people in discovering who they are, determining what inspires and drives them, and overcoming limiting ideas. His approach clarifies what one wants in life, assisting people through goal-setting and a step-by-step process for achieving them. He empowers people to make deliberate and responsible decisions, allowing them to identify their blind spots and evolve as individuals via the use of numerous strategies and tools.

The foundation's bold, uncompromising, and compassionate ventures are always aimed at initiating the "Inner Transformation" process. They focus on spiritual growth, personal growth, and self-healing while emphasising that true progress lies in "Inclusive Growth and Co-existence." This philosophy drives all their initiatives, encouraging a holistic approach to development and well-being.

Under Shree Shambav's leadership, the foundation has launched several impactful movements:

Shree Shambav Green Movement: This mission is to create a healthy, green, and clean earth through responsible water conservation and greening initiatives. The movement strives to make the world a green paradise by encouraging sustainable living and environmental responsibility.

Shree Shambav Vidya Vedhika (Vizhuthugal): This project aims to help students and children by offering training, books, stationery, and uniforms. It aims to provide the next generation with the tools and resources they need to excel both academically and personally.

Shree Shambav and his foundation exemplify the spirit of compassion, transformation, and inclusive growth via their work, which has a profound impact on individuals and communities around the world. His work exemplifies the power of acknowledging and nourishing the human spirit, creating a world in which everyone can reach their full potential and appreciate the beauty of life.

TESTIMONIALS

Journey of Soul - Karma - "We die in our twenties and are buried at eighty." Remember that nothing can stop someone who refuses to be stopped. "Most people do not fail; they simply give up." Shree Shambav deserves full credit. It allowed me to sit and consider what I might miss out on in life. The author has delved into every aspect of our daily lives. How can a seemingly insignificant change in these seemingly insignificant details bring us such joy? The Soul of Journey teaches you the "art of living" as well as the "art of dying."

Twenty + One Series - The rich cultural heritage offered a host in twenty + one short stories with incredible imagination, morals and values prevalent at a given time, influencing how people respond to a crisis or any situation. The author has recreated images with universal values and morals. The plentiful of fascinating from faraway lands would leave the modern play and story writers a cringe. The book supports trust and immeasurable values instilling hope for the new generations.

Death - "Shree Shambav's 'Death - Light of Life and the Shadow of Death' is an extraordinary masterpiece that delves deep into the profound questions surrounding our existence and mortality. The book's opening statement, 'Nothing ever truly dies; it simply ceases to exist in one form before resuming it in another,' sets the stage for a thought-provoking exploration of death's multifaceted nature. Shambav's remarkable ability to navigate the philosophical complexities of death and our universal fear of it is both enlightening and comforting. This book is a testament to the power of understanding and acceptance."

Whispers of Eternity - "Reading 'Whispers of Eternity' by Shree Shambav was a transformative experience that left me captivated from beginning to end. Each section of this exquisite collection delves into the myriad facets of existence, offering poignant reflections on life, death, and everything in between. Shree Shambav's verses are a testament to the beauty of language and the power of expression, inviting readers to embark on a journey of self-discovery and spiritual awakening. Whether celebrating life's simple joys or grappling with the complexities of human emotion, this book is a timeless companion that speaks to the heart and soul of every reader."

Life Changing Journey Series - "Life Changing Journey Series II Inspirational Quotes" is a remarkable collection that illuminates the path to self-discovery and personal growth. With its inspiring quotes and insightful reflections, this book serves as a beacon of light in a world often shrouded in darkness. Each quote offers wisdom, guidance, and encouragement, reminding readers of their inner strength and resilience. A must-read for anyone seeking inspiration and enlightenment.

Learn To Love Yourself – "A Heartfelt Guide to Authentic Self-Love." "Learn to Love Yourself" invites readers on a transformative journey to embrace their true essence in a world often focused on external validation. Through ten insightful chapters, it gently reveals principles of genuine self-love, guiding readers to deepen their connection with themselves. Beyond surface positivity, it encourages the cultivation of resilient self-acceptance, from embracing one's unique qualities to setting empowering boundaries. With inspiring stories and practical wisdom, this book is a trusted companion on the path to inner peace, fulfilment, and joy, helping readers build lives that reflect their authentic selves.

The Power of Letting Go – This book has been a gift to my spiritual journey. Shree Shambav's insights into attachment, personal growth cycles, and forgiveness are enlightening. The concept of seven-year cycles resonated with me, helping me understand the natural phases of life. I feel more empowered to let go of what no longer serves me and step into a life of freedom and fulfilment. A truly beautiful read!

A Journey of Lasting Peace – "A Journey of Lasting Peace" feels like a trusted friend guiding you through the maze of self-discovery. The 18 transformative principles are both practical and deeply resonant, addressing everything from gratitude practices to the art of letting go. Each chapter is infused with warmth and wisdom, making it easy to apply the concepts to my life. I particularly appreciated the emphasis on physical health's connection to mental well-being; it served as a wake-up call for me to prioritize my health. This book is an invaluable resource for anyone serious about personal growth!

Astrology Unveiled Series – "Profound, Logical, and Inspiring". What stands out in Astrology Unveiled is the author's dedication to making Vedic astrology logical and approachable. Each concept flows naturally into the next, backed by examples and exercises. The insights into karma and life cycles add a philosophical depth rarely seen in astrology books. Perfect for anyone seeking spiritual growth alongside astrological knowledge!

The Entitlement Trap - "Thought-Provoking and Challenging" The book challenges readers to confront their own sense of entitlement, and that's not easy—but it's essential. The Entitlement Trap doesn't offer a one-size-fits-all approach. Instead, it's a thoughtful, layered examination of how entitlement can limit our growth. The chapter on "Defining Your Own Hill" was particularly impactful, as it pushed me to reconsider which challenges are truly worth pursuing. A thought-provoking read for those willing to do the inner work to create a life they can be proud of.

Whispers of a Dying Soul – "A Soul-Stirring Reflection on Life's Unspoken Truths" - *Whispers of a Dying Soul: Unspoken Regrets and Unlived Dreams"* is a deeply moving exploration of the unexpressed emotions and unfulfilled aspirations that shape our lives in ways we often don't realise. This book invites readers to confront the powerful, often hidden impact of regret while guiding them through a journey of introspection and healing. Each page opens a space to reflect on the choices that define us—from moments of unspoken love to neglected passions—offering a gentle reminder to live authentically and courageously.

Whispers of the Soul: A Journey Through Haiku - is a mesmerising collection that speaks directly to the heart. Each haiku is a delicate brushstroke capturing life's fleeting beauty and timeless wisdom, inviting readers into moments of deep reflection and peace. This book is a balm for the soul, guiding us to find meaning in stillness and connection in simplicity. The themes of nature, love, and mindfulness echo universal truths, resonating with quiet, powerful grace. It's a book to be savoured slowly, cherished deeply, and returned to often. Truly, a gift for anyone seeking calm and clarity in life's chaos.

Whispers of Silence - Unlocking Inner Power through Stillness by Shree Shambav is a rare gem that beckons readers to pause, reflect, and reconnect with their inner selves. In a world that never stops talking, this book offers a profound exploration of silence—not as a void but as a rich and transformative space.

From the first page, Shree Shambav's writing resonates deeply, blending scientific insights with spiritual wisdom in a way that feels both universal and deeply personal. The author's ability to bridge the tangible and the transcendent makes this book an invaluable guide for anyone navigating the chaos of modern life.

The Power of Words: Transforming Speech, Transforming Lives - "The Power of Words is a profound and enlightening guide that has transformed the way I approach communication. Shree Shambav masterfully uncovers the hidden influence of our words on relationships, self-perception, and overall well-being. This book doesn't just teach you how to speak; it inspires mindful communication that fosters connection and trust. The insights on replacing negative patterns like gossip and judgment with kindness and authenticity are truly life-changing. The practical strategies and engaging narratives make it an invaluable resource for personal and professional growth. A must-read for anyone striving to communicate with intention, clarity, and compassion. Highly recommended!"

The Art of Intentional Living: Minimalism for a Life of Purpose - "The Art of Intentional Living is a refreshing guide to finding clarity in a cluttered world. With practical wisdom and profound insights, it inspires you to simplify, prioritise, and live with purpose. A must-read for anyone seeking balance and fulfilment."

Awakening the Infinite: The Power of Consciousness in Transforming Life - "Awakening the Infinite is a transformative guide that expands the mind and nourishes the soul. With profound insights and practical wisdom, this book beautifully explores the power of consciousness, helping readers connect with their true purpose and inner potential. It is a journey of self-discovery, healing, and spiritual awakening, offering clarity and inspiration at every turn. A must-read for anyone looking to live with greater awareness, meaning, and authenticity."

ACKNOWLEDGEMENTS

To my grandfathers, grandmothers, mothers, fathers, aunts, uncles, neighbours, sisters, brothers, friends, and teachers, they poured in endless moral stories, retellings of Ramayana, Mahabharata, Puranas, Upanishads, and so on.

My teachers, neighbours, and kindred souls. Who provided us with a stage to perform wonderful Puranic stories and were gracious enough to acknowledge our efforts.

The artists and translators of epics have served as a source of inspiration, invigorating our spirits, making these works accessible, and enabling us to grasp the profound depths and deeper dimensions they contain.

I also cherish the stimulating conversations; I had with my wonderful mothers, Punitha Muniswamy and Uma Devi.

Our family's youngest member, Aadhya, who always overwhelmed me with questions, inspired this book.

I would likewise prefer to express gratitude to Mr Sivakumar, Mrs Roopa Sivakumar, Mr Akshaya Rajesh, Ms Akshatha Rajesh, Ms Apeksha Prabhu, Mr

Akanksh Prabhu, Mr Nikash Sarasambi, Mrs Spoorthi Nikash for their valuable inputs.

I must thank Mr Rajesh, Mr Savan Prabhu, Mrs Revathi Rajesh, Mrs Rajani Sarasambi, and Mrs Manju Reshma, who encouraged me and often suggested writing a book. Their unwavering belief that I had something valuable to offer kept me going during my writing sessions.

Love you all,

Shree Shambav

www.shambav.org

shreeshambav@gmail.com

BOOKS BY - AUTHOR

Journey of Soul - KARMA

"Journey of Soul – Karma" is a heartfelt exploration of life's profound truths in our increasingly complex world. Addressing challenges, inequalities, and the quest for meaning, this book brings the timeless concept of Karma into focus. It emphasizes Karma not merely as philosophy, but as a guiding principle for our daily lives, inspiring us to walk a path of integrity and purpose. Through this journey, readers gain insights into how actions shape destinies, encouraging a life aligned with truth and compassion. It's a beacon for those seeking a deeper, more fulfilled existence.

Death - Light of Life and the Shadow of Death

In *Light of Life and the Shadow of Death*, the enigma of mortality is approached with clarity and compassion. Death is an inevitable certainty, yet it casts a lingering shadow of fear over our lives, stirring grief and despair as we strive to prolong our time on earth. This profound work examines the fate of departed souls and the heavy emotions we attach to loss. Yet, it offers a path toward accepting death and finding peace amid life's uncertainties. Exploring our origins, ethical values, and purpose, it unveils the sustaining truth of existence. The shadow of death, though daunting, is reframed as a shared, universal experience—one that calls us to confront our deepest fears with wisdom and grace.

Whispers of Eternity 150 Plus - A Symphony of Soulful Verses

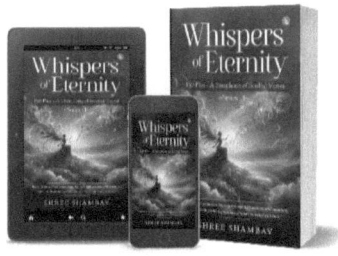

Step into the soul-stirring world of *Whispers of Eternity* by Shree Shambav, a collection of over 150 poems that capture the essence of the human experience. Divided into sections like "Through the Seasons," "Whispers of Hope," and "Threads of Unity," the book journeys through life's phases, emotions, and the universal connections that bind us all. Shree Shambav's verses touch upon nature, love, and spirituality, inspiring readers to find beauty in the everyday. Each poem is a finely crafted reflection, rich with insight and depth. *Whispers of Eternity* invites readers to pause, reflect, and embark on a timeless journey through the landscapes of the heart and soul.

Life Changing Journey Series I and II

In Life Changing Journey - 365 Inspirational Quotes Series I, Shree Shambav curates a powerful collection of 365 original quotes across fourteen chapters, each crafted to touch the heart of our daily lives. More than a simple compilation, this series speaks directly to personal experiences with wisdom and depth. Quotes like, "The most beautiful things are unseen but can be felt," echo the quiet beauty of life's intangible moments. Another, "Giving up is easier; holding oneself up is wiser," provides a guiding light in challenging times. Life Changing Journey reveals the transformative power of carefully chosen words, inspiring readers to find strength and new perspectives on their paths. Through Shree Shambav's work, readers are reminded of the wisdom and resilience hidden within each day.

Twenty + One - 21 Short Stories Series I and II

In *Twenty + One - Short Stories*, Shree Shambav brings to life the often-overlooked characters of nature—trees, animals, and mountains—revealing their intrinsic worth beyond mere utility. With poetic personification, he gives voice to these silent beings, some of whom are lucky enough to have names, titles, and rare human protection. Mountains, usually seen as mere landmarks, are depicted with reverence, emphasising their enduring presence. The stories build a bridge between humans and the natural world, showing that pain, grief, and resilience are shared across all forms of life. Shambav invites readers to empathise with the silent struggles of trees and animals, inspiring a fresh perspective on ecology and our responsibility towards the environment. This collection is a call to honour our connection to nature, encouraging readers to foster compassion and respect for all life.

Learn To Love Yourself

Learn to Love Yourself is a powerful invitation to turn inward in a world focused on external validation and superficial measures. Through ten transformative chapters, each offering a key rule for self-love, readers are guided to uncover their inner beauty, cultivate personal strength, and develop a solid foundation of self-acceptance. This journey goes beyond momentary happiness; it's about building an authentic relationship with yourself that fosters resilience, joy, and fulfilment. From embracing your unique qualities and practising compassion to setting boundaries and pursuing what makes you come alive, this book provides essential insights and practical guidance. Let *Learn to Love Yourself* be your trusted companion on this path, inspiring you to unlock the limitless potential within and find true inner peace.

The Power of Letting Go

The Power of Letting Go invites you to release attachments, fears, and expectations, guiding you toward true inner freedom and joy. With deep insights, practical exercises, and timeless wisdom, this book equips you to face life's challenges with resilience and grace. It explores the essence of attachment, embraces the power of seven-year growth cycles, and teaches the art of forgiveness as a key to a fulfilled life. Each chapter brings concepts to life through relatable analogies and real stories, making profound ideas both accessible and engaging. Let this book serve as your beacon for self-discovery and spiritual awakening, helping you navigate uncertainties and unlock your potential for a joyful, meaningful existence.

A Journey of Lasting Peace

A Journey of Lasting Peace is a transformative guide to self-love, inner peace, and personal strength, where Shree Shambav leads readers through 18 powerful principles for discovering their true selves. Each chapter explores vital themes, from the quest for inner peace and the importance of self-awareness to the healing practices of mindfulness and yoga. Through practical strategies, reflective exercises, and heartfelt stories, this book offers a clear roadmap to a more authentic and fulfilling life.

Whether you seek to embrace imperfection, establish healthy boundaries, or reconnect with nature, A Journey of Lasting Peace provides the wisdom to navigate life's challenges and find enduring tranquillity. Perfect for anyone on a journey of self-discovery, this inspiring work gently reminds us that lasting peace starts within.

Astrology Unveiled: Series I and V

Astrology Unveiled: Foundations of Ancient Wisdom invites you to unlock the mysteries of astrology, offering timeless knowledge rooted in the teachings of ancient sages. This comprehensive guide explores fundamental principles like Rashi, Graha, Bhava, and Divisional charts, making it an essential resource for beginners and intermediate students alike.

With logical explanations and practical applications, Shree Shambav skilfully blends ancient insights with modern understanding. Rich in examples, detailed explanations, and engaging exercises, this book serves as an illuminating path to mastering Vedic astrology.

Embark on a transformative cosmic journey, discovering how astrology can unveil your destiny, guide life's choices, and support your spiritual growth.

The Entitlement Trap: Get Over It, Get On It

Are you feeling stuck in a cycle of blame and dissatisfaction? The Entitlement Trap: Get Over It, Get On It offers a transformative path to reclaiming your personal power. This insightful guide helps you break free from the mindset of victimhood and empowers you to take control of your life. Inside, you'll discover how to redefine success, prioritize your true values, and live with purpose. Through practical strategies, you'll learn to embrace simplicity, connect with nature, and leave a lasting legacy. Get ready to shift from powerless to empowered and create a life you love!

Whispers of a Dying Soul: Unspoken Regrets and Unlived Dreams

"Whispers of a Dying Soul", embarks on a profound journey that delves into the silent longings we often carry but seldom express. This powerful exploration uncovers the unspoken emotions that shape our lives—missed opportunities, unfulfilled dreams, and the quest for authenticity. Through heartfelt reflections and transformative insights, this book invites you to confront your regrets and turn them into powerful catalysts for growth and healing.

Whispers of the Soul: A Journey Through Haiku Series I to IV

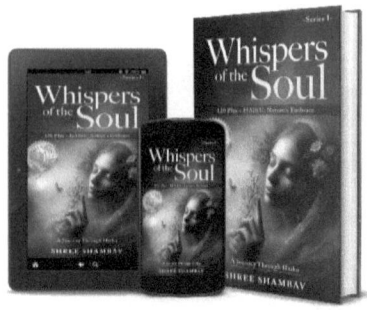

"Whispers of the Soul: A Journey Through Haiku" is a poetic invitation to pause and rediscover life's hidden beauty. This transformative collection of haikus explores themes of nature, mindfulness, love, and the human journey, offering profound reflections on universal experiences. Divided into five series, the book delves into nature's elegance, the depths of inner stillness, the tenderness of human connection, the passage of life's seasons, and the mysteries beyond the self. Each haiku captures fleeting moments with timeless grace, guiding readers toward peace, self-discovery, and a renewed appreciation for life's simplest wonders. This is more than poetry—it's a soulful journey.

The Power of Words: Transforming Speech, Transforming Lives

The Power of Words: Transforming Speech, Transforming Lives, illuminates the profound influence of our everyday language. This book explores how words can heal or harm, connect or divide, urging readers to embrace mindful communication. It delves into the "Sins of Speaking," such as gossip and judgment, while celebrating virtues like honesty, kindness, and authenticity. With practical strategies for transformation and a focus on the art of listening, Shree Shambav offers a roadmap to elevate our conversations. Perfect for both personal growth and professional development, this guide inspires readers to use their words to create peace, foster deeper connections, and lead a life of integrity and purpose.

The Art of Intentional Living: Minimalism for a Life of Purpose

In a world that celebrates more, The Art of Intentional Living invites you to embrace less. This powerful guide explores how minimalism can transform every aspect of your life—your space, your time, and your mind—by removing distractions and focusing on what truly matters.

Through simple yet profound principles, you'll learn to:

- Declutter your physical and digital space
- Prioritise what aligns with your values
- Create time for meaningful connections and experiences
- Cultivate a life of purpose, peace, and clarity

Awakening the Infinite: The Power of Consciousness in Transforming Life

In a fragmented world, Awakening the Infinite explores the power of consciousness to heal, transform, and unite. This book takes you on an experiential journey, revealing how awareness shapes reality and connects us to universal wisdom. Through spiritual teachings, introspection, and practical insights, it helps you uncover your soul's true purpose. Transformative practices, guide you toward emotional healing, clarity, and personal growth. As you deepen your awareness, you'll forge a profound connection with yourself and the world around you. Embracing this journey leads to a life of mindfulness, authenticity, and purpose. Ultimately, it is an invitation to awaken the infinite potential within.

www.ingramcontent.com/pod-product-compliance
Lightning Source LLC
LaVergne TN
LVHW091705070526
838199LV00050B/2288